INTERVIEW STRONG

GET THAT JOB CHANGE YOUR LIFE

Your Ultimate Employment Coach:
Empowering Job Interview Techniques
Customized Résumé Essentials
Learn the Reason They Hire You

MARK JONATHAN

Interview Strong

Paperback ISBN: 978-1-7372229-1-0
eBook ISBN: 978-1-7372229-0-3

Author Contact: mj@37bridges.com

Professional editing by Editing Alchemy
Editor Contact: ktreellc@gmail.com

Proofreading by Heather Randall Editing
Proofreader Contact: heather@hrandallediting.com

Internal Artwork by Zoe Judge
Contact: jayjzoe@gmail.com

Book design by TeaBerry Creative
Contact: tara@teaberrycreative.com

For my family and the Five,
who I love and who are strong.

INTERVIEW STRONG
IS YOUR ULTIMATE EMPLOYMENT COACH.

Throughout this book I will teach you how to prepare for and ace that job interview. Whether you are a college graduate looking for your first job, experienced and looking for your next move, or need to reinvent yourself and your career, this book is for you.

WHO IS MARK JONATHAN?

- Senior executive in human resources
- Twenty years' experience
- Selection, hiring, and talent acquisition
- Seasoned interviewer and interviewee

WHAT YOU WILL LEARN

- Essential Preparation
  - » *Interview mindset and process*
  - » *Big T Factor—why they hire you*
  - » *Awesome resume design*
  - » *What to wear and why*

- Empowering Interview Techniques
  - » *Hit Backs and Double Punches*
  - » *Directional Targeting*
  - » *Win Tough Questions*
  - » *How to Talk Money*
  - » *Closing and Following Up*

CONTENTS

ORIGINS

Employment is key in maintaining your dignity, independence, and financial self-reliance.

This section, inclusive of chapter one, is the *Interview Strong* backstory. If you would find that boring or need to get right into the techniques and skills, you can immediately jump into the methodology, beginning in chapter two.

THE END OF A JOB, THE BEGINNING OF A QUEST

I never saw it coming. It hit me with an all-encompassing force—stunning, penetrating, sweeping my feet out from beneath me. Illogically, it felt freeing in the moment. The impact was tempered by the actuality that the shock waves would not truly hit me until later in the game. The real crucible was time, and the clock commenced ticking upon the termination of my employment.

Ironically, the end of my job was a euphoric release from the day-to-day grind. Feelings of freedom and transformation rushed into and frolicked about in my mind entertaining my imagination. However, those visionary sails filled with the breeze of sea change were quickly surpassed by waves of financial stress, which morphed into storms of monetary terror.

I became a reluctant conscript of unemployment, enlisted into the unanticipated competition of getting a job.

The unemployment experience was like a personal earthquake to my life, shaking me out of my comfort zone and thrusting me forward through difficult times and into unanticipated experiences and foreign destinations.

The realization that my financial demographic was changing as an effect from my unemployment hit next. I had missed the memo on that makeover.

I was so busy trying to maintain it all that I was in denial of the fact that my financial deficit train was leaving the economic station.

I had not reserved a seat on that train, but I was learning that such a seat was mandatory for the unemployed. The ride was rough and the scenery new. I saw savings drain. Homeownership morphed into renting. The inevitable juggling of bills to make ends meet caught up with me at a pit stop at a dark and lonely station.

The scenic route on my runaway economic train also encapsulated personal stretching—the kind of stretching that extends to finding self-worth when what had defined me for so long was now gone. The stretching went so far as to include discovering self-confidence in the face of rejection.

I had to stretch further to develop powerful customized resumes that would unlock doors to interviews and to develop unique and powerful interview skills to beat out the competition and **get that job.**

If you are unemployed and feel like no one really understands you, I can tell you this: I absolutely know and understand what it is like to walk through the trial of unemployment. It is truly hard on many fronts.

Unemployment crept up on me, catching me napping, my eyes focused on work, blind to my industry bubble bursting.

> *Not in my wildest imagination did I*
> *ever see myself being unemployed.*

I was, of course, very naive on that point. I was comfortable and conditioned by a technology industry with high demand. Looking back, I was also insulated in my own confidence that my feet were on indestructible ground, the kind of ground bolstered up by a profession, a good education, and solid work experience. Either way, my unemployment earthquake left me stranded.

> *I can attest that the hand of unemployment*
> *touches every aspect of your life, and its*
> *long, boney fingers are very unforgiving and*
> *reach very sensitive personal places.*

Over time the experience became highly impactful. I worked on job applications during the day and reviewed bills and bank balances at night. I started to feel the budget bite, and the teeth were razor sharp. Shopping centers, once a place of enjoyment, now became taxing. I began to dread Christmases, birthdays, and other celebratory events. My family's needs, initially placed on the back burner, started to burn bright, and the job search became more desperate.

My bank balance was not the only balance that drained downward. My dignity and confidence also took a hit. Each unsuccessful application drained my feeling of personal worth.

> *I confess, I started to feel like a real loser,*
> *like no one wanted me. And trust me, that*
> *is not a good mindset to be in, especially*
> *when you need to keep job interviewing.*

I had to develop and apply internal soul anchors to keep and maintain my personal worth and confidence so that I could *Interview Strong.*

I had to find and hold on to my intrinsic value in the face of rejection. My refining experience of unemployment taught me that it was vital to strengthen both soul and skills in order to *Interview Strong.*

It was difficult to know which way to begin as I tried to balance getting a job in my current career with getting just any job. It was hard to know if I should stay the course and keep applying to jobs aligned to my experience or go off-road, follow a path of desperation, and take any job.

Either way, I believe in the principle that when
one door closes another door will open.

I learned to trust in that principle and not to be afraid of opening new doors and going off-road. If you hold experience in an industry and there is demand for jobs in that industry, staying the course is often best. For me, I had to adapt, change, and move into a different industry. I learned not to be afraid to change and move. I believe that you can also change and move to a new career if needed.

You can redevelop yourself to survive and
find new success in a different career.

One aspect of my unemployment journey was that I often felt alone—very alone. I had never contemplated the power and effect employment could have upon social status.

My awareness was increasing that unemployment can be a small hinge on which the social door can swing, and that door can shut sharply. Critical judgments carelessly carry your name on the wind, while whispered conversations effortlessly arrest your reputation.

Maybe people did not know how to help. Maybe they felt I was accomplished enough to not require help. Maybe they did not want to feel obligated. But I was alone.

Maybe you also feel alone in your unemployment?
I hope this book helps you to not feel alone anymore.

I can attest that a core emotion that seeds from being unemployed or underemployed is the feeling of rejection. That core feeling that no one wants you strikes at the heart of your dignity.

The challenge is to not let unemployment
rob you of your dignity.

It does not matter if you are a recent graduate who knows the new stuff or a seasoned pro with experience. Day after day your soul, your dignity, your confidence can be eroded by the rejection inherent in unsuccessful job applications.

What defines your success is elusive, and that is hard, but not impossible, to navigate.

It is vital to preserve your dignity
and personal worth.

My unemployment experience became a great teacher in maintaining personal dignity. That hard time in my life also significantly built up my resume muscle and developed my interview strength, skills, technique, and strategy.

The experience also taught me that interview
skills and your soul, your dignity, are
interdependent, that both skills and soul need
strengthening in parallel to Interview Strong.

I have often been asked how I maintained my dignity, confidence, and self-worth through my unemployment experience.

What did I learn from interviewing for jobs, and how did I refine and build strong interview skills?

Answering these questions and outlining solutions is my purpose for publishing *Interview Strong*.

Through my unemployment journey, I commenced building an index of interview skills and techniques that were strong and effective, and I have refined them over the years. I started to apply these skills and techniques in interviews. Many of these skills and techniques are contained in this book and are foundational to the *Interview Strong* methodology. Following my execution of what I now call the *Interview Strong* skills and technique, the floodgates opened, and I received several offers. It was like a monsoon after a long, hard drought.

On my journey back to employment, I also encountered unemployment's ugly cousin, underemployment. I know firsthand how having this cousin sitting beside you at work and staying at your house can feel. I know what it is like to work below your potential. It can be difficult to swallow. That kind of daily digestion gives you indigestion. What should you do when you are in such a position? How should you react? I will cover answers to these questions in upcoming chapters.

I was once asked what the core difference is between being unemployed and underemployed.

I answered that both unemployment and underemployment are hard and threaten your dignity. Unemployment is just more terrifying.

I jokingly say that I am the spy within. After years of working as a senior human resources executive, I know what the employer is looking for and how the interview and selection process is managed. Conducting countless interviews, scanning resumes, and reading cover letters over the years has given me the ability to professionally job coach you via this book.

My current career in and years of human resources experience, combined with my past personal experience of unemployment, form a powerful duo of real-world experience. That kind of capability enables top professional skills and expertise to help you successfully overcome unemployment and **get that job**.

I bring a magnified empathy and understanding and an undeniable skillset to the table.

I have written *Interview Strong* with the intent to help job seekers gain employment or improve their underemployment faster and more effectively.

This work and methodology, these skills, techniques, ideas, and principles, are solely mine. I have lectured on the *Interview Strong* methodology over the years and have consulted and job coached.

I believe the *Interview Strong* methodology to be a very powerful toolkit. I believe this work will help people successfully build tremendous job interview skills, techniques, and resume design capability. I also believe this methodology will help people strengthen their interview skills by maintaining their soul, their dignity.

My goal is to help people approach interviewing with strong skills and an empowered mindset and soul and thereby achieve a significant advantage.

> *My message is that you and I can*
> *triumph over our job derailments.*

I hope my past difficult and very challenging experience of unemployment, combined with my years of professional human resources experience, can count for something. I hope my experience can count to help you and many others struggling in unemployment or underemployment to **get that job** and succeed.

My favorite saying is "A job can change a life."

> *Interview Strong.*
> *Get that job and change your life.*

INTERVIEW SKILL
AND TECHNIQUE I

You should be Really Interview Ready
in order to *Interview Strong*.

Most candidates do not develop their interview skills and technique despite working hard for weeks to win that job interview. That is mind-blowing to me.

CHAPTER TWO

THE *INTERVIEW STRONG* INTERDEPENDENCY MODEL

Candidate Number Four provided an insightful moment in a windowless conference room. I noticed immediately the soul of the man. The way he carried himself, his walk, his swag. All of the non-verbal's loudly screamed, "I am unemployed, and no one wants me!" Rounded shoulders and a heavy character sunk into the chair. As the interview progressed, Candidate Number Four's interview skills were traditional but somehow lacked effectiveness. I could tell Candidate Number Four felt marked by his unemployment and that the crucible of time had eroded his confidence. Consequently, I could see that Candidate Number Four's diminishing dignity was negatively impacting his capability to *Interview Strong*.

My heart ached for Candidate Number Four. Unemployment was inhibiting his ability to *Interview Strong*, and his demeanor was creating doubt within me as an interviewer. Could he pass an interview with management? I was not sure. I studied him carefully.

My eyes discovered a perfect reflection of a younger me emerging within Candidate Number Four. It was a memory moment—a depiction of me, years ago, back in my crucible of unemployment. The self-portrait was revealing, even raw, and definitely not flattering.

The haunting, unresolved emotions that held me captive back then during my experience of unemployment danced and galloped on the human canvas of Candidate Number Four.

I wished in that moment that I could help Candidate Number Four. "If only I could reach him," I thought. "Shake him to realize his true worth; wake him to hold onto his dignity, to hold his head high and not feel diminished by unemployment!"

Candidate Number Four had my compassion, but he also had my renewed realization of the impact unemployment can have on our dignity, on our soul.

CANDIDATE NUMBER FOUR NO MORE

Candidate Number Four's last employment had abruptly ended one morning, without warning, following years of dedicated service. The termination had been shocking and brutal.

But Candidate Number Four had not strengthened nor healed his soul and, as a result, was struggling to interview. Undeveloped, mediocre interview skills and technique were not helping. Candidate Number Four needed strengthening in both soul and skills to *Interview Strong*.

> *Overall, Candidate Number Four's resume read like an obituary.*

It was not a resume that was customized to sell him for this job. Rather, it was a eulogy resume of his last job.

Eulogy resumes are the worst type of resume. They showcase the job you did for the last ten years that is now shockingly dead. A eulogy resume is an easy error to make but also an easy mistake to correct.

My summary of the experience was categorically this: there should be no Candidate Number Fours!

THE *INTERVIEW STRONG* INTERDEPENDENCY MODEL

The *Interview Strong* methodology introduces to you the *Interview Strong* Interdependency Model as the first concept.

This model illustrates that in order to *Interview Strong*, interview skills and soul are interdependent yet impact and rely on each other. Both your interview skills and your soul require dual parallel strengthening. I firmly believe that the degree of strength in your soul—your dignity, personal worth, and self-confidence—will impact the effectiveness of your interview skills. Likewise, weak, and inadequate interview skills and technique will not save the interview for you, even if you are strong in your soul, dignity, personal worth, and self-confidence.

> *Many people do not prepare for their hard-won job interview by developing their interview skills, technique, and soul. That is mind-blowing to me!*

Many candidates just review interview questions and suggested responses from the internet, despite working hard for months to get that interview. That approach is counterintuitive to me and, at its core, self-jeopardizing.

In my experience, you should develop interview skills and a technique that can be summarized in an interview strategy and plan and then be executed in your interview. Why? So that you can be prepared to perform at your very best and give yourself every chance to **get that job**.

I also believe that you need to have strengthened your soul in order to be interview ready, especially because unemployment can strike at the heart of your dignity. Your personal worth and confidence require soul anchors to hold you fast against the storms of rejection inherent in the interview selection process.

Both soul and skills work together and combine in strength to help you Interview Strong.

One evening, I was contemplating how to teach the connection and interdependency between **soul**—how you think and feel—and **skills**—your interview skills and technique. This is the structure of the *Interview Strong* methodology, and I needed a way to demonstrate it.

On a break, I picked up an hourglass, and the sand inside transferred back and forth between the two bubble ends as I turned the hourglass upside down and back and forth. As I observed the fluidity of the sand, I realized I had the perfect model in my hand. To me, the movement of the sand between the two bubble ends of the hourglass demonstrated extremely well the connectivity between skills and soul. I could use the hourglass to help teach the concept to candidates, to help them strengthen both skills and soul in order to achieve optimal interview performance.

Building interview skills and technique is essential. However, I believe you will not be totally effective without strengthening your soul, especially if unemployment has impacted your dignity.

To me, both soul and skills may need different levels of strengthening at any given time. Many interview methods singularly focus on interview skills. The *Interview Strong* methodology focuses on strengthening both skills and soul in parallel for optimal interviewing effectiveness and performance.

I believe if your interviewing skills and technique are weak, but your soul is strong, you will likely ooze a confident demeanor but will be ineffective in your interviewing capability and performance. If your interview skills and technique are strong but your soul is weak, the results achieved from the execution of your high interview capability will be diminished by your demeanor and interpersonal vibes.

In my experience, unresolved feelings, diminished dignity, reduced confidence, or double mindedness will inhibit and reduce the effectiveness of your interview skills and technique.

The emotional side of unemployment is like the thorn in the lion's paw. It is the silent inhibitor, and a lion cannot hunt effectively with a thorn in its paw.

Soul inhibitors can include financial hurt from your unemployment experience or injured feelings that come from rejection. Employment challenges really strike at your dignity. Soul inhibitors can be emotions or adverse feelings from the last negative job experience or ongoing hurt from that job you were unfairly let go from.

Soul inhibitors impact the interview in many ways. Primarily, they dam the flow of your interpersonal skills, which are key in holding conversations necessary to Interview Strong.

To achieve optimal interviewing effectiveness and *Interview Strong*, both soul and skills need to work together in dual strength and capacity.

One bubble end of the model hourglass exemplifies interview skills; the other exemplifies soul. You can buy an hourglass and place it somewhere visible to remind you of the principle of building both skills and soul to *Interview Strong*.

In this book, the two Interview Skill and Technique sections present supporting role-plays that teach you the *Interview Strong* methodology and help you interview more effectively.

The Resume Design section is crucial to helping you draft and build an awesome resume.

To help you get interview ready in your soul, there are two sections on Soul Anchors. As you read these, reference the hourglass model often to reinforce in your mind the interdependency of soul and skills and how together they enable you to *Interview Strong*.

In this book you will also find tools like the You Matrix, which helps you find new personal content for your resume.

You will also find a core chapter on how to talk about money.

This book begins by teaching you interview skills and techniques like the Interview Mindset, the Big T Factor, and the *Interview Strong* technique. You will learn Hit Backs, Double Punches, and Directional Targeting that you can execute in your interview.

Then you will advance to chapters that focus on elements of the soul, like Soul Essentials and Soul Tactics, to help you prepare your soul to take those interviews head-on and be at your very best. These soul chapters are designed to reduce soul inhibitors and enhance the effectiveness of your interview skills.

You will also read about what I call the What to Wear Factor.

Finally, you will find chapters on how to Close Out an interview and follow up.

Chapters on Tough Questions are also included to help turn difficult interview questions to your advantage.

I have incorporated all I can in *Interview Strong* to empower you to have stronger job applications, to interview more effectively, and to ultimately **get that job** and change your life.

CHAPTER THREE
INTERVIEW MINDSET

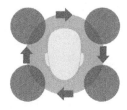

Congratulations—you landed a coveted job interview! It took more time and effort than you thought it would. Countless hours of searching and numerous job applications have finally secured you an interview. Fantastic! You have researched the company, dressed impeccably, and are on your way to arrive early to the interview. This is all awesome. However, are you Really Interview Ready?

Say what?

Are you Really Interview Ready? Think about it. On average, you will be one of nearly one hundred applicants who applied and one of maybe twelve to fifteen who were shortlisted for an interview.

Again, are you Really Interview Ready?

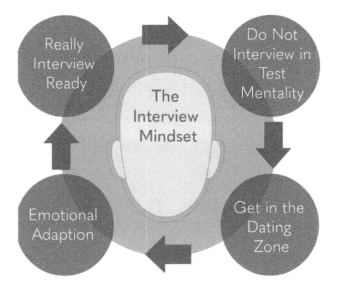

To get an interview takes a lot of work, time, and effort—usually weeks, if not months, of work, many applications, and networking initiatives. After all that work and effort, it amazes me that the average candidate will proceed to an interview with zero or minimal preparation when it comes to developing their interview skills and technique.

In my opinion, going online and researching the top fifty interview questions and practicing suggested answers, will not cut it. That kind of interview skill and technique preparation is not what I would call being Really Interview Ready.

Limited preparation will almost certainly be counterproductive to your results, especially if the interviewers are experienced.

Professional interviewers will quickly work their way behind your memorized answers. Good interviewers are like bears and will smell out your lack of substance, and their teeth and claws will be razor sharp. It will be embarrassing for you but fun for interviewers. You will have a bad day for the rest of the day. The next day you will need to restart job application work because you were not Really Interview Ready. On average, it will take at least another month of applications before you get another interview.

Would it not have been better to have worked hard on your interview skills and technique and been Really Interview Ready to win that interview?

To be Really Interview Ready, you need to build capability before your interview to ensure your skills and technique are refined, practiced, and ready to execute. A customized interview strategy and plan will also greatly help you to gain the highest ratings possible. I cover interview skills and technique as well as designing your interview strategy and plan in upcoming chapters.

To be Really Interview Ready also includes being prepared for Tough Questions and knowing how to leverage advantage from those questions.

My purpose is to help you win the interview prize you have fought so hard to get and be really ready to *Interview Strong*.

DO NOT INTERVIEW IN TEST MENTALITY

I was staying at The Grand America Hotel in Salt Lake City. It is an amazing hotel—one of my favorite hotels in the world. The lobby is remarkable, with exquisite charm, marble, and wood layers. Late one night I could not sleep. (I am not sure why because the rooms and beds are so amazing.) I took a stroll down to the lobby. It was peaceful. I had become acquainted with one of the doormen. He was completing his studies in finance, commencing interviews with investment banks, and working the hotel doors at night to make ends meet. Given his impending interviews, I took some time to help him.

He confided in me that he felt like vomiting at just the thought of going in for a job interview. I was intrigued. I pictured him interviewing with investment bankers, armed with a vomit bucket.

I asked why he felt like vomiting. He looked at me legitimately puzzled, as if I were naive to what was on the line with his upcoming job interviews.

"Well," he continued, "I get so nervous."

"What makes you so nervous?" I inquired.

He looked at me, puzzled. His eyes searched me for understanding. He explained that to him, every interview question was like an exam question. Consequently, the pressure upon him to pass the interview test was enormous. No wonder he was going to projectile vomit.

> *I had seen this approach and reaction numerous times before. Many candidates approach an interview this way, with an Interview Mindset that I call Test Mentality.*

I said, "Okay, so you are making one of the biggest mistakes job candidates make in job interviewing." I had his attention.

Curious, he asked, "What do you mean?"

His posture straightened, more posed for action rather than defeat.

"Have you ever ridden a horse before?" I asked. He indicated that he had. I said, "Well, you are too tight in the saddle. You cannot ride a horse like that. You are too tight in the saddle for a job interview, and it will not work for you. They will not hire you because you are not going to interview well." I continued, "For you that would be a shame, because you are a great candidate."

I could see he was good talent. He would be a great employee for an investment bank.

*However, his Interview Mindset would
mask his talent as he interviewed.*

I could see that his Interview Mindset was also creating nervousness that would camouflage his real value. He would be too tight in the saddle, and that would all culminate in killing his chances of getting hired.

"Test Mentality is the wrong approach to a job interview for you," I said. "You are thinking about it the wrong way. It is not a test. Approach the interview that way and you will significantly reduce your interview performance."

He was riveted in what I was saying to him.

He asked me, "How do I make that change?"

I said, "Well, you are married, right?" I had noticed his shiny wedding band.

"Yes," he said.

I asked him to tell me how he met his partner, how long they had dated, and how he proposed. They had a great love story.

Then I asked, "So did you feel like vomiting when you proposed?"

"No," he said, "Not at all, of course not."

I asked, "Why not?" He went on to indicate that he knew it was right, that he and his partner had talked about moving forward together before proposing, and that he felt comfortable in asking the big question.

I said, "So for the biggest interview of your life—proposing—you were not nervous?" I continued, "That's good. Approach the job interview exactly like that." I said, "Approach the interview like it's a date, not a test. Listen, I have had a lot of experience with this over the years," I reinforced.

"The biggest mistake candidates make, is framing the interview in their mind and in their approach as a test, and then executing the interview accordingly."

I pushed further, "You were not nervous to the point of vomiting when you proposed because you didn't approach it like a test. As a result, you were your best self." He got the principle.

I call this ineffective approach and frame of mind interviewing in Test Mentality. This approach is exemplified by going to the interview with the mindset that it is an exam to pass, preparing and approaching each interview question as if it were a test question.

Do not interview in Test Mentality

Over the years I have observed that interviewing in Test Mentality generally causes you to be too tight in the saddle. It can be hard to think clearly under Test Mentality, and you will likely treat each question like a mini exam, giving your best answer as if ticking off items on a shopping list. Most candidates then breathe a sigh of relief after each question and wait in silence for the next question.

*Interviewing in Test Mentality also causes
you to Interview Assumptively.*

Interviewing Assumptively is when you do not have clarity into the intent of the question. When you Interview Assumptively, you are never sure what ratings you scored from your answer. You are much like a blindfolded tennis player, serving with great effort and hoping the serve lands in the right area of the tennis court.

*Interviewing Assumptively is not a good
way to play tennis or interview.*

Interviewing in Test Mentality also inhibits you from achieving the Big T Factor, which is why employers will hire you. I want to help you cultivate that factor. We will cover Big T Factor in upcoming chapters.

*For now, it is key to understand that it is
ineffective to interview in Test Mentality and
minimizing to Interview Assumptively.*

Do Not Interview in Test Mentality
- It places you under test pressure.
- You will be too tight in the saddle.
- You will Interview Assumptively.
- You will inhibit the Big T Factor, the factor that determines if employers will hire you.

GET IN THE DATING ZONE

I often say to candidates, "You are going on an interview date." I reinforce the dating approach to job interviewing because it is a helpful antidote for interviewing in Test Mentality.

Get in the Dating Zone. Interview the employer
as much as they are interviewing you.

This mindset gives power back to you. This is a healthy adjustment and realization for most candidates. Approaching a job interview in Date Mentality also empowers you to be more genuine and less nervous.

Approaching a job interview in Date Mentality is also a mindset of mutuality: an interview is a mutual opportunity to get to know each other. A motivating factor that I like to teach candidates at this point is the reality of employer expectations. Understanding the employer–employee relationship helps candidates to maintain a Date Mentality mindset. For my college graduate friend in the lobby of The Grand America Hotel, this part of the conversation went like this:

"Listen, you need to go and date the employer. You need to find out what their culture is like, what they value and do not value. It is time to get to know them to determine your compatibility."

Then I hit him with the leverage factor to help transition his interview mentality from test to date. I said, "Here are some employment realities. First, they are going to work you like a dog." I had his attention. "They are going to want you in the office early in the morning and, depending on the culture, you can either leave with the fear of death at 6:00 p.m. or with a degree of management approval at 9:00 p.m." I added, "They will also expect performance. You will likely be measured by return and profitability on customer accounts."

I continued, "These performance expectations will likely differ between firms and will be tempered by management. Your boss will determine your day-to-day reality. Company policy and culture will drive your life." I paused and let these realities sink in. I could see his mindset adjusting.

I will teach further interview skills and techniques in upcoming chapters to empower you to not interview in Test Mentality. For now, understanding the realities of employment relationships will help you transition out of Test Mentality and into Date Mentality.

> *Date Mentality also creates the perfect setting to cultivate the Big T Factor, which is why employers will hire you.*

In my experience, Test Mentality inhibits the Big T Factor. Date Mentality facilitates it. The Big T Factor, why employers hire you, will be covered in the next chapter.

For now, remember:

- A job interview is like going on a date.
- Ensure you have a Date Mentality mindset. An interview is a mutual opportunity to get to know each other.
- Understand the realities of the employment relationship: it is one of hard work, and you will have to perform.

EMOTIONAL ADAPTION

Emotional Adaption is going into your interview having a mindset ready for change. This is generally a significant part of your interview preparation. If you are not emotionally ready to adapt, to change your job or career, or to move to something new, it will be discernible to interviewers and will affect your interview performance.

> *I have seen candidates not advance through the selection process simply because they were not emotionally ready to adapt.*

To me, Emotional Adaption is non-negotiable. The opposite mentality and behavior to Emotional Adaption, of course, is resistance or inability to make changes in your work.

Inability or resistance to change in your work can manifest in many ways. Examples are; inability to move on from what you did for the last ten years, difficulty in changing position or title, unwillingness to relocate when needed, struggle to move to a different role, reluctance to change industries or transfer to a new specialization, and struggle to accept a lower title or reduction in pay when that is the best option.

Can you interview enthusiastically for an entry level advertising position even though you just graduated and see yourself as an advertising senior executive?

- Can you change industries?
- Can you move on to something new?
- Can you take a pay cut to survive?
- Can you relocate if needed?

It is imperative to have Emotional Adaption embedded in your mind and heart, especially if the job you are interviewing for requires change in career plans, seniority, or salary expectations.

You should accept the change brought to bear upon your job life prior to your interview.

An important aspect of Emotional Adaption is accepting rejection. Candidates I have coached have a common reaction to rejection—they take it very hard. I pick them up and dust them off and say, "Don't worry about it. Not a big deal."

Not understanding me, they respond, "What! Did you not hear what I just said?"

My reply is simple. "Yes, I understand. Your reaction is positive. You are heading in the right direction."

They are usually stunned by my response. "What do you mean?" they ask.

That is when I reinforce the principles of Emotional Adaption in dealing with rejection:

- Rejection is a friend in disguise.
- Accepting change includes accepting rejection.
- A rejection confirms that the job was not for you and that you are closer to the right job.

A job is key to your dignity, self-reliance, and independence. Understanding this empowers you to develop Emotional Adaption.

> *We may need to accept different work to move forward and maintain our dignity.*

- Accept change in your work life.
- Be ready and willing to embrace change prior to interviewing.
- Emotional Adaption is crucial because a job is core to your dignity, independence, and self-reliance.

CHAPTER FOUR
THE BIG T FACTOR

Employers will be looking to hire the best. But what does "the best" mean? Take a step back and think about this. Generally, many candidates, usually hundreds, will apply for a job.

Utilizing resumes, employers will shortlist approximately twenty candidates for phone screening interviews, which they will then cut down to around ten candidates to come in for in-person interviews. By this stage, it is highly likely that all the candidates will be similar in terms of the minimum qualifications—education, experience, and required skills to perform the job. There will likely be some variance among the shortlisted candidates in years of experience and breadth of skills and likely some personality uniqueness around fit to culture. After the next cut, candidates will likely be even more similar. Then, following the second round of interviews, it comes down to the final three candidates. There is now significantly less difference between the finalists. Who is the best candidate?

WHY EMPLOYERS WILL HIRE YOU

To manage the selection process, job criteria is used to protect against adverse selection. That is, candidates are rated by interviewers against job criteria to eliminate discrimination and bias. Job criteria is a safe zone for selection decisions as it is based on independent business criteria for the position, not personal interviewer bias.

The last time I checked, human beings are interviewing and ranking candidates. Therefore, can personal bias be totally ruled out? What drives interviewer ratings? What determines the best candidate? What drives the core hiring decision? I believe, from years of experience in human resources, the answer to that question is what I call the Big T Factor.

Over the years, I have learned
that people hire who they trust the most.
That is what I call the Big T Factor: Trust.

Why is trust such a key factor? Think of all the interdependencies that intersect at trust. To start with, it takes a great amount of trust to hire you.

Management hires who they trust the most to:

- Get the work done effectively.
- Represent the company.
- Engage with clients and customers.
- Lead staff and teams.
- Manage financial responsibilities.

An additional, often overlooked reason that trust is crucial in hiring is the unmistakable fact that the decision to hire you says something about who selected you.

> *Have you ever thought about that?*
> *You reflect upon the person who hires you.*

The decision to hire you will be immediately evaluated by associates, peers, downline reports, and upper management. The assessment of your hire is immediate upon introduction, and assessment will be recurring. The assessment will not necessarily be formal, and it will mostly occur through first impressions. Your interpersonal skills, how you introduce yourself, how you hold yourself, how you engage in the work, and early indications of results will either confirm your hire decision or will send up red flags.

The water cooler talk will either boil over with frustration about you or bubble with positivity. The ultimate return on the risk to hire you will of course be determined by longer-term results.

But for now, you are under first impression investment and return scrutiny.

If you have children or a four-legged adorable best friend and are looking to hire a babysitter or petsitter, who will you choose? Let us say you have three candidates in front of you. Let us say after your search and selection that all three final candidates have similar qualifications. There are, of course, some differences in experience, personality, and maybe varying degrees of fit to your family culture or your pet's personality. But ultimately, who will you hire to look after your beloved children or pet?

I put it to you that after interviewing the candidates and weighing all the factors on your list, you will hire the babysitter or pet sitter you *trust* the most.

You will not hire someone you do not trust.

I have managed employees over the years, and I can tell you, as a senior human resources executive, that I can manage staff performance, overlook minor flaws, and develop skill gaps. But if I cannot trust an employee to represent me in their daily interactions, in their comings and goings, it is almost impossible to continue the employment relationship.

Why? *Because trust is at the core of the employment relationship.*

If I cannot keep a current employee who I do not trust, how on earth can I hire a candidate who I do not trust?

Candidates who understand that the Big T Factor is core to being hired will understand how vital it is to gain and build trust in an interview.

> *Smart candidates will therefore change how they interview to gain trust. They will adopt skills and techniques to increase their Big T Factor.*

The intent and design of the *Interview Strong* methodology is to help you increase your Big T Factor, to give you every possible chance to win the interview and **get that job**.

CHAPTER FIVE

INCREASING YOUR BIG T FACTOR

I am standing in the center of a lecture theater stage with a bunch of tennis balls in my hands. The hall is full of college students eager to learn interviewing skills. Attendees are intrigued. They came to learn how to get a job, not to learn how to play tennis or win Wimbledon!

I ask an attendee an interview question and throw a tennis ball at them. They catch it. They answer the question. I ask another question and throw another tennis ball. They catch it again. After several more questions and tennis balls, the attendee starts to find this process taxing.

> *They will immediately start to*
> *interview in Test Mentality.*

By the seventh question and ball, the attendee is trapped, interviewing in Test Mentality. One question follows another, and the attendee does not have time to think or prepare for the next question. The attendee starts to drop the tennis balls, and they roll all over the lecture hall.

TENNIS LESSONS

Interviewing in Test Mentality is not the attendee's only problem. They are now also Interviewing Assumptively.

The attendee is answering each question the best they can. They are hoping that they have correctly understood the context and intent of the question and that their answer is hitting the target, but they are not sure.

A candidate in this interview situation is truly Interviewing Assumptively. They are listening to questions with assumptive intent and responding to each question accordingly.

By this time, the attendee is struggling to hold on to all the tennis balls, but the green missiles keep coming.

The tennis balls continue to drop and roll all over the lecture theater. This picture is truly symbolic of what generally occurs when a candidate interviews in Test Mentality and as a result is also Interviewing Assumptively.

When candidates Interview Assumptively, they achieve hit and miss ratings.

The consequence of interviewing in Test Mentality and Interviewing Assumptively is a reduction in your Big T Factor.

In the traditional interview process, the candidate does not initiate any opportunity to get behind the question, to ascertain the real intent of the question.

When interviewing under the traditional interview process, for the majority of the time you are not doing anything to increase your Big T Factor other than to give your best answers.

> *Interviewing Assumptively is akin to gold mining with no strategy: digging where the guy in the hat tells you to, throwing up mounds of earth, and hoping for gold in each shovel load.*

From experience, I have learned that if you follow the traditional interview process, it is also common to prepare by memorizing answers from an internet search on the top fifty interview questions. You will not only interview in Test Mentality and Interview Assumptively, but you will now regurgitate memorized answers disingenuously. If your interviewers are experienced, this will generally culminate in doubt in you. It will inhibit your Big T Factor and risk you not getting the job.

QUESTION AMBIGUITY

What other insights did you pick up from the tennis lesson?

An interview question is designed to measure or determine skill, experience, or knowledge and to ascertain abilities. These measurements are assessed from your response to interview questions within several minutes. What makes the task of answering interview questions even more difficult is that often, many interview questions are drafted poorly or are worded without professional research.

Many interview questions are poorly framed and ineffective in measuring the real intent of the question.

This all culminates in poor quality assurance for the question design and answer measurement.

I was once part of an interview selection panel for an administration position. Management needed a candidate with the ability to deal with unwanted intruders who appear without an appointment. The position worked in an area of shared service administrators.

The interview question was framed to determine and measure the candidate's ability to deal with any unwelcome intrusions and was worded as this: "How well do you deal with conflict?"

I was surprised at the drafting of the question. I was even more astonished as each candidate answered the question regarding how well they handled conflict with peers. The general answer was, "I get along really well with others, and especially with my peers. If there are any differences, I simply address and resolve them."

Remember, the question was seeking to assess how well candidates would manage employees demanding to see management, not conflict with peers.

> *It was fascinating to me that not one candidate asked what type of conflict the question was assessing, nor did the interviewers provide any clarification.*

Candidate responses were accepted and rated accordingly. As a result, each candidate was rated poorly to moderately on this question.

> *I have noted this experience time and time again in interviews over the years.*

I have seen many ill-framed questions mislead candidates in their responses or cause candidates to miscue the real intent of the question.

> *More importantly, candidates who clarified the question—which meant getting behind the question and establishing the core intent of the question—generally performed better.*

Why? Because, in my observation, candidates who got behind the question were able to ascertain the real business reasons driving the question. That information is gold and enabled candidates to provide an additional response to fully answer and satisfy the question.

Clarifying the question, or what I call executing a Hit Back—getting behind the question to confirm the real business drivers that produced the question—is a powerful technique to develop and execute in a job interview.

Hit Backs are a potent skill to safeguard you from interviewing in Test Mentality and from Interviewing Assumptively. Hit Backs also empower you to increase your Big T Factor.

GETTING BEHIND THE QUESTION

I firmly believe you should hit the "interview question ball" back to the interviewer. One of the best techniques to do this is to Hit Back by asking clarifying questions and generating a discussion to build your Big T Factor.

The basic idea of the Hit Back technique is to ask clarifying questions that help you understand the core intent of the question and the associated business drivers behind the question.

Hitting Back enables you to sell yourself for the real intent of the interview question and demonstrate a higher fit for the job.

Hitting Back the question also provides you time to think before responding. Those thinking seconds can be vital for you and, as a result, can help lift your interview performance.

The Hit Back technique also transforms a percentage of the interview into a conversation and thus prevents you from interviewing in Test Mentality and from Interviewing Assumptively.

Remember, from my experience, employers hire who they trust the most. Holding a conversation with them will help build that trust.

HIT BACKS

On average, you will have an hour to build trust during an interview. This means that you generally cannot Hit Back every question.

Plan to Hit Back and get behind approximately sixty to seventy percent of the interview questions.

Your interview strategy and plan should ultimately determine what questions you are going to Hit Back and why. I cover interview strategy and plan in chapter 7. But for now, I recommend that you explore and master Hit Backs to give you every opportunity to increase your Big T Factor.

I have included the following role-plays that demonstrate the Hit Back skill and technique.

Interviewer: How do you handle conflict?

Candidate Hit Back: Can I ask, what kind of conflict are you referring to—internal with peers or external with customers?

Interviewer: Internal. In the past we have had a lot of trouble with this position being able to handle conflict with production staff.

Candidate Additional Hit Back: Thank you. What has caused the conflict with production?

Interviewer: Tell us about yourself.

Candidate Hit Back: Personally, or professionally?

Interviewer: Professionally.

Candidate Hit Back: Tell me, what is it that you are most interested in regarding my professional background?

Interviewer: Well, we just wanted to get to know you, but given that you have asked, we are really interested in your track record in sales growth and your closing ratios.

Interviewer: What is your greatest strength?

Candidate Hit Back: I have several key strengths. What area of strengths are most important to you for this position?

Interviewer: Can you tell us about your account management experience?

Candidate Hit Back: Certainly. I have over ten years in account management. It is my passion, and I love it more than anything except my spouse and dogs Zeus and Apollo. Can you tell me—what are the two major capabilities that you are looking for in account management for this position?

Interviewer: We are really looking for someone who can cross-sell in boardroom presentations when we conduct product reviews. Secondly, we are looking for a top closer.

Interviewer: What kind of presentation experience do you have?

Candidate Hit Back: Presenting is a talent I have developed. I absolutely love presenting. Before I explain further, what kind of presentation skills are key for this position?

Interviewer: We do a lot of presentations to executive committees on our products and implementation process.

Candidate Hit Back: Is there anything different in your presentation process from the normal industry standards?

Interviewer: Yes, we highly value the ABC presentation methodology.

These are good examples of solid Hit Backs! As you can see, Hit Backs are a proactive technique that allow you to ascertain the core intent and business drivers of the question.

Interviewer responses to your Hit Backs will generally provide you with good insight to clarify what the employer is really looking for. You can then use this information to affirm your fit and increase your Big T Factor in responding further to the question.

Please note that you can utilize additional Hit Backs to make sure you get right to the core issue of the question.

Sometimes it can take several
Hit Backs to strike gold.

Remember, ambiguity is alive and well in interview question land. By Hitting Back, you can eliminate that ambiguity.

Once you receive clarifying information from
interviewers, you can then use that knowledge
to formulate an on-target response I call a
Double Punch, which I will cover later.

For now, what if you miss that Hit Back in the interview because you were nervous? Or what if, just out of habit, you answer the question before executing a Hit Back? I want to ensure you that you can always execute a strong Hit Back.

HIT BACK CHASERS

There is a solid technique to recover Hit Backs that I call Hit Back Chasers. The technique is simply to perform a Hit Back immediately following your best first answer.

This is a good technique to learn. The following are some role plays that exemplify Hit Back Chasers.

Interviewer: How do you handle conflict?

Candidate best answer: Well, I am not afraid of conflict; I just face it and handle it to a resolution.

Candidate Hit Back Chaser: Can I ask, what kind of conflict are you referring to? Internal with peers or external with customers?

Interviewer: Tell us about yourself.

Candidate best answer: Well, I have been working for CDE company for the last three years, and I really need a change. When I saw your posting, I thought that this is a high fit job for me.

Candidate Hit Back Chaser: Can I ask, in telling you about myself, what information would you like me to focus on?

Interviewer: What is your greatest strength?

Candidate best answer: My strengths are in account management and closing sales.

Candidate Hit Back Chaser: But I do have several more key strengths. Can I ask, what areas of strength are most important to you for this position?

Interviewer: Can you tell us about your account management experience?

Candidate best answer: I have ten years of account experience, and I am passionate about delivering service and growing sales.

Candidate Hit Back Chaser: Can you tell me, what is it that you are most looking for regarding account management experience?

Interviewer: What kind of presentation experience do you have?

Candidate best answer: Presenting is a talent I have developed over the years. I absolutely love presenting. I am well skilled in board presentations and executive summaries.

Candidate Hit Back Chaser: Before I answer further, are there any skills or audience-specific presentation experience for this position that you are looking for?

HIT BACKS, FIT, AND TIMING

Not every interview question can or should include a Hit Back. Hitting back every interview question would likely come across as odd.

*Not all interview questions require Hit
Backs to increase your Big T Factor.*

The most common questions I receive when teaching the Hit Back technique is:

- How often should I Hit Back?
- Which interview questions should I Hit Back?
- Are there interview questions to Hit Back that are more important than other questions?

I believe you should learn and practice the *Interview Strong* skills and techniques and do your best to naturally execute them in your interviews. This kind of approach will enable you to interview sincerely and will help the skills and techniques to be part of your character rather than a facade.

*I suggest that candidates Hit Back approximately
sixty to seventy percent of the interview questions.*

I believe if you can do that you will be balanced in your approach and will significantly increase your overall interview performance. A good indicator of success is that you have hit the question ball back enough to result in a conversation for over half of the interview.

Ultimately, when you become proficient at developing and following a customized interview strategy and plan, that plan will provide you a strategic road map to determine the following for each interview: when to Hit Back, what questions to Hit Back on, and why it will provide you advantages to Hit Back when you do.

HITTING BACK THE RIGHT TENNIS BALLS

Not all interview questions are equal. Some interview questions are more important than other questions in the interview question lineup.

What makes an interview question stand out for a Hit Back?

The answer is the basis of the question.

Questions based upon core job criteria are high priority questions that you should aim to Hit Back. Peripheral questions to the core job criteria are less important.

Job postings outline the core job criteria. Start with the job posting to help identify the most important interview questions to Hit Back.

Once you have identified the core job criteria, you can prepare Hit Backs for questions that will target core job criteria. You can rate the core job criteria by importance to help you determine the priority Hit Backs.

The key is to save and target your Hit Backs for the interview questions that focus on essential job criteria.

After delivering a solid Hit Back and receiving confirmation of the real intent of the question, what are you going to do?

You are going to increase your Big T Factor by immediately following up with an awesome response that targets what the employer is really looking for. The next technique is designed to help you do exactly that, helping you to hit the question out of the ballpark for a home run. I call this the Double Punch.

DOUBLE PUNCH

The Double Punch acts as a follow-up combination after a Hit Back. A Double Punch is a quick, powerful, two-reason response to the information received from a Hit Back. Use a Double Punch immediately after your Hit Back is answered by the interviewer.

To get hired, you need to sell yourself.

I refer to this technique as a Double Punch because it identifies two selling points about yourself based on the new information obtained from your Hit Back. Two reasons are stronger than one.

A Double Punch should validate that you are a strong fit for what the employer is looking for.

Some answers may require a triple punch. That is okay. The rule of thumb is a Double Punch, but if you need to, you can always sneak in a third punch. Why not? But in my experience, a Double Punch is generally adequate.

DOUBLE PUNCH: IN AND OUT IN SIXTY SECONDS

The best Double Punches are executed in sixty seconds or less. Practice delivering your Double Punches in sixty seconds so that you can deliver them effectively and increase your Big T Factor. I want the best results for you with your Double Punches. The punchier and more concise, the stronger the impact.

The language of a Double Punch should be like your knuckles—hard, powerful, and straight to the point.

The biggest challenge I have in teaching candidates the Double Punch is to help them see that often, less is best.

I believe the natural human tendency for job interviewing is to focus on more is best. That is, the candidate will seek to jam in as much content as they possibly can in their answer to the question.

Less is best, is a hard concept for most people to accept when executing their Double Punches.

To reinforce the idea, less is best, I ask candidates to think of one of their favorite movie lines, a killer line that just stays in the mind.

The one-liner sticks more readily in the mind than any essay ever will.

It takes practice for most candidates to be direct and concise in delivering their Double Punches. Most candidates are trying to condense down their memoirs to two knuckle-sized statements. But once they achieve a Double Punch in under sixty seconds, it gives them power.

The power of the Interview Strong technique is magnified when Hit Backs combine with Double Punches to clearly sell yourself against the core job criteria.

In delivering your Double Punches, you do not want to hit the wrong target.

When you add the fine art of Double Punch Prep Statements to line up your Double Punches and include that skill in your *Interview Strong* technique, I believe it will change your interviewing forever.

*Like sizing up your opponent and lining up
your strikes, you need to achieve the same
skill in delivering Double Punches.*

Let us move to the next set of role-plays to exemplify the additional techniques of Double Punch Prep Statements and Double Punches.

Interviewer: How do you handle conflict?

Candidate Hit Back: Can I ask, what kind of conflict are you referring to—internal with peers or external with customers?

Interviewer: Internal. In the past we have had a lot of trouble in this position with conflict among production staff.

Candidate additional Hit Back: Thank you. What has caused the conflict with production? Is it coordination of sales or some other issue?

Interviewer: Coordination of sales.

Candidate Double Punch Prep Statement: I appreciate the clarification. I have never had difficulty with production in coordinating my pipeline sales. It has never been an issue to me, and I believe I can provide more context and insight on this point to answer the question fully:

First Punch: I believe in partnering with production, as I have always built a partnering relationship with production. I will eliminate and address any conflict casual to my sales coordination.

Second Punch: I also hold a proven track record in coordinating my sales regularly with production to ensure I absolutely meet their cycle needs.

Candidate further Hit Back: Can you tell me if this approach matches your company culture and processes?

Interviewer: Absolutely. That is exactly the kind of approach we are looking for. However, we have introduced an online tool to enable managers to update daily.

Candidate Double Punch Prep Statement: Any input or reporting requirements you give me in the role I will absolutely meet because I am well experienced in utilizing online tools. I also feel it important to add:

First Punch: I will exceed your expectations in getting reporting submissions in on time every day.

Second Punch: I have a proven track record in timely reporting and accountability no matter the process or software.

In the previous examples, the candidate took approximately sixty seconds for their Double Punches. In doing so, they increased their chances to significantly boost their Big T Factor on this question.

Imagine if the candidate had just answered the question following the standard interview process, given their best answer in Test Mentality, and Interviewed Assumptively.

Here is another example of how to execute effective Double Punches.

Interviewer: Tell us about yourself.

Candidate Hit Back: Personally, or professionally?

Interviewer: Professionally.

Candidate: I have over eight years' experience in IT account sales. Selling and account management is my passion. I am a ninja closer, relationship-builder, and sales growth guru.

Candidate Hit Back: Tell me, what is it that you are most interested in regarding my professional background?

Interviewer: Well, we are really interested in your track record in sales growth and your closing ratios.

Candidate Double Punch Prep Statement: My track record speaks for itself in sales growth, and I love to speak to it, too. It is my passion to grow market sales. Some examples I would like to speak to are:

First Punch: I have consistently delivered account growth for every account I have managed. My last two accounts grew from twenty percent to over forty percent.

Second Punch: My closing ratios are awesome! Closing ratios have been delivered at over eighty percent in the last three years running.

Candidate Hit Back: Can you tell me about the product support you provide?

Interviewer: [Talks at length about the amazing product support they have.]

Candidate Double Punch Prep Statement: That is wonderful. I feel that I have high compatibility with your support and culture.

First Punch: I can see myself working extremely well with your product support.

Second Punch: I have always maintained a close relationship with product support and marketing, and I will continue to do that if you hire me.

This question was turned into a Big T Factor gain. On average, other candidates would have answered the question, unsure of whether they hit the target and intent of the question or not.

Here is another example.

Interviewer: What is your greatest strength?

Candidate's best answer: My greatest strength is account management and growing accounts to achieve maximum market penetration.

Candidate Hit Back Chaser: Although I have several key strengths, before I share more, can I ask, in what area of the job are personal strengths most important to you?

Interviewer: Well, the job has a huge customer-facing requirement, which we are most interested in.

Candidate Additional Hit Back: Oh, I see. I love the customer-facing piece. What is it in customer-facing that the company really needs in your operations today?

Interviewer: We really need people who can face and resolve customer complaints without getting frustrated and follow them through to the very end. We want a total closeout without any loose ends.

Candidate Double Punch Prep Statement: I know from experience that my strengths are in customer-facing and follow-up. Let me explain:

First Punch: I do not get angry at customers with complaints. I have fully accepted that customer complaints are part of the job.

Second Punch: I also work by a saying: "It is not done till it is done." If I am handling a complaint and lose the customer off the line, I will contact them. I never closeout a complaint until the resolution is complete.

Interviewer: Thank you.

The candidate potentially turned a high-level strengths question into a drill-down, *Interview Strong* situation, achieving as much of the Big T Factor classic as they could.

Interviewer: Can you tell us about your account management experience?

Candidate Hit Back: Certainly. I have over ten years' experience. Account management is my passion. Can you tell me, what is the major capability that you are looking for?

Interviewer: Well, we are really looking for someone who can cross-sell in board room presentations when we do product reviews.

Candidate Double Punch Prep Statement: That is helpful. I am so passionate about cross-selling. I want to provide some further insight about me in regard to cross-selling:

First Punch: I have successfully achieved a lot of cross-selling in the past, with product A to products B and C.

Second Punch: It is not covered in my resume, but I thrive in cross-selling, especially in the boardroom product review environment. I was a lead in cross-selling in my previous position.

The candidate is out with a stronger performance than what would have been achieved if they had followed the standard interview response—not to mention the incremental gain in their Big T Factor. It is noteworthy that in this example, the candidate was able to cover the point of being a lead for cross-selling, which was not included in their resume and was not clear in the job posting.

Here is another example.

> **Interviewer:** What kind of presentation experience do you have?
>
> **Candidate Hit Back:** Presenting is a talent I have developed. Before I explain further, what kind of presentations are key to the success of this position?
>
> **Interviewer:** We do a lot of presentations to executive committees on our products and implementation process.
>
> **Candidate Further Hit Back:** Is there anything different in your presentation process from the normal industry standards?
>
> **Interviewer:** Yes, we utilize the ABC methodology.
>
> **Candidate Double Punch Prep Statement:** That is perfect. I have over five years' experience in presenting products in this industry. But I want to reinforce to you that:

First Punch: I am fully capable of using presentation software; they called me a guru in my previous role. I also have eight years' experience presenting to executives.

Second Punch: I also have a lot of exposure to the ABC methodology. I know it is extremely effective, and I cannot wait to use it. I was aware that you utilize the ABC methodology, so I commenced a course in it.

The candidate is out with a high chance of increasing the Big T Factor on this question.

THE DATE SCENARIO

Now that you understand the basics of Hit Backs, additional Hit Backs, Hit Back Chasers, Double Punch Prep Statements, and Double Punches, I want to help you achieve additional depth in the *Interview Strong* technique with a fun going-on-a-date scenario.

I am going on a date. There have been some get-to-know-you touchpoints. There is mutual interest. My date and I are meeting at a café for lunch and to engage in get-to-know-you chat. As we talk, my date asks me a question.

"What do you think about art?"

I can jump to a lot of assumptions at this point in my response. I could respond, "It is so boring."

If my date is an art lover, with a response like that the date could be over before it begins, and I will end up eating lunch alone. If my date is an art lover and I also like art, I would want my response to be different and to inject mutuality. Either way, I still might be missing the essence of what my date does or does not like about art. It could be that they do not like the fact that art is not accessible to the masses, or they might hold reservations regarding the cost of art today.

If I want to increase my chances for a second date, I need to get behind the question to ensure the proper context of the question, to get an understanding of the core intent and personal drivers of the question. Without that, I am dating in Test Mentality and also Interviewing Assumptively.

If I answer on assumption, I may strike out; I may miss. I may never know why there was no second date. If I want to have another date, I need to demonstrate my compatibility, my alignment to what my date is looking for in regard to art.

I need to be sincere, or I will be embarking upon a process of manipulation, which will not work in the long run for anyone. But clearly, it is time now for Hit Backs, additional Hit Backs, Double Punch Prep Statements, and some fast and furious Double Punches.

I excuse myself and quickly slip out to the bathroom, kick off my shoes, adorn my martial arts robe, put on my black *Interview Strong* belt, add a sweat-resistant headband for good measure, and head back out to my date. I mentally prepare a Hit Back right up front. No Hit Back Chasers on this date. I want a second date, so I am going in strong.

Back at the table, I unleash a fast and effective Hit Back with my right hand as I reach for a chip and dip with my left.

"On your question regarding art. Well, for me, it depends. Can I ask, what is your philosophy regarding art?"

My date answers, "Well, I love modern art, but I just don't like historical art. It is too old for me."

My Hit Back has provided me with good understanding and insight that I did not previously possess. I did not realize the important distinction of the variable between modern and historical art for my date. I can now respond further with alignment to build the Big T Factor.

Double Punch Prep Statement: I also personally just cannot get into the old historical art. I cannot relate to it.

First Punch: I actually really love modern art and bold lines.

Second Punch: Nothing makes a room pop more than the right piece of modern art.

My date nods in agreement and smiles. I can get behind the question even further. I Hit Back again with the speed of a leopard but the elegance of a gazelle.

"Do you just like modern art paintings, or do you also have a leaning toward modern art pieces for furnishings?"

My date replies, "I like modern art in terms of art paintings, but I really like photographs of people—raw images of life on the walls. And most of all, I love modern pieces to furnish a room."

Now is my opportunity to seal the deal, to gain the Big T Factor. Double Punch time. I need to sell myself, my alignment, my compatibility in under sixty seconds. Remember, identifying two aspects is stronger than one. I respond, very quickly, with two selling-in testimonials of me. My Prep Statement will line up my punches.

Double Punch Prep Statement: Oh, yes. I mean, the right piece can really make a room, right?

Next, I deliver the Double Punches after a quick sip of my sturdy bubbling mineral water to calm the nerves.

First Punch: I absolutely agree with you that I really think modern art pieces are the way to go to furnish a home. There is nothing better than coming home to cool modern pieces.

Second Punch: I also love pictures on the walls that are real. I have framed photos all over my pad of friends, family, and memories. I do not like the commercial pictures.

This is a great example of the *Interview Strong* technique in practice via a date frameup.

It is best to be sincere, or you will be manipulating. In this case, if you are not being honest, your consequence could be ending up living in a home with a partner you love but surrounded by modern art pieces you despise. Now, if you can live with that tradeoff, then okay. But if that outcome would be negative, then do not falsely align with your Double Punches. If you are saying it, you need to stand behind it or be able to live with the tradeoffs.

Practice your Hit Backs, Hit Back Chasers, Double Punch Prep Statements, and fast and powerful Double Punches.

Practice is the key to becoming empowered and accurate with your Hit Backs and Double Punches in a real-life job interview.

You will be surprised at how quickly you become confident and highly skilled in interviewing with the *Interview Strong* technique. I believe you can get to a proficient level that allows you to increase your Big T Factor, handle almost every interview situation, and interview more empowered than you ever have before.

You really can Interview Strong.

CHAPTER SIX
DIRECTIONAL TARGETING

Professional tennis players are amazing to me. Their speed and power in striking the ball back to their opponent is awesome. What really impresses me is their ability to hit the ball with Directional Targeting. They hit back strategically to spread their opponent across the court, drop it short, bring their opponent to the net, or keep their opponent on the baseline. It is easy to just play tennis; it is a step-up technique to hit back with the power and agility of Directional Targeting.

My next objective is to have you master the *Interview Strong* technique of Directional Targeting.

Directional Targeting is the ability to identify three to five Interview Court Hot Spots on the interview court.

*Interview Court Hot Spots are peripheral
criteria that can impact your interview ratings.
They are areas the employer values highly
that you can address during the interview
to gain incremental Big T Factor points.*

Interview Court Hot Spots are usually not expressly included in the core job criteria but may be included, known, or cited as secondary, important, or valued requirements.

You execute Directional Targeting as you maneuver interviewers to Interview Court Hot Spots and hit additional points home. The purpose of Directional Targeting is to help you increase your interview rankings and ratings.

The power of the Directional Targeting technique is magnified when combined with Hit Backs, Hit Back Chasers, Double Punch Prep Statements and Double Punches.

INTERVIEW COURT HOT SPOTS

When I role-play this technique with college students, at first their Directional Targeting efforts can be a bit humorous. However, when I respond as an interviewer and chase them down, they suddenly realize they can get caught without direction.

*You can use Directional Targeting to
achieve very clear, strategic outcomes.*

My daughter Brooke was preparing to interview for an internship. I asked her what her plan was for Directional Targeting and provided some coaching.

She had her Hit Backs and Double Punches planned to cover core job criteria, but she had not planned any Directional Targeting to encapsulate all of the criteria and important attributes that would be highly valued by the employer.

I said, "Brooke, the pool of candidates for that internship will be highly competitive, and you are going to need every edge you can get."

I have seen candidates win jobs simply because their Directional Targeting efforts got them over the finish line by a toe when the race was neck and neck. After several coaching sessions, Brooke had her Directional Targeting ready. She *Interviewed Strong* and got the internship!

Our coaching sessions to prepare her Directional Targeting went like this:

"Brooke, tell me about the employer."

She explained that they were a legal firm, prestigious and professional.

I asked what she would be doing in the internship day-to-day.

Brooke indicated that she would be assisting with drafting legal briefs, performing research, and assisting attorneys.

I said, "Brooke, if you were them, what else would you be looking for in a candidate other than the core job criteria?"

I continued, "You can cover core job criteria with your Hit Backs and Double Punches, but what else will be very important to them that may not be expressly covered in their question lineup?" I ventured further, "What will be their Interview Court Hot Spots on the interview court?"

We discussed what we concluded would be the firm's perspective in terms of the "complete package" that the employer would value highly in an intern.

In other words, we defined their additional important and high-value criteria.

Brooke had also networked with a previous intern, and her networking efforts had given her insight and information. She learned that the firm liked interns who took initiative and who worked independently. Brooke also learned that the firm wanted interns who were skilled in writing and managing projects.

However, none of these Interview Court Hot Spots were in the job criteria.

While planning out Brooke's Directional Targeting, we landed on several Interview Court Hot Spots:

- High working independence
- Writing expertise
- Project readiness

We also decided to include Interview Court Hot Spots for maintaining confidentiality and good citizen behavior, as we felt that a law firm would also value these standards very highly.

I said, "Brooke, they do not want anyone who will breach their clients' confidentiality. They will be looking for someone who possesses maturity and understanding when it comes to maintaining confidentiality."

I then moved on to good citizenship. I said, "They will also not want a party animal who will cause them problems after hours. After all, you will represent the firm twenty-four seven."

We ended up with five Interview Court Hot Spots for her Directional Targeting, which I will cover next.

At this point in the preparation process, I encourage candidates to not only name these Interview Court Hot Spots but also to extrapolate them out into concise action statements. For Brooke, the action statements looked like this:

- Independent worker that gets the job done.
- Awesome writer who eats briefs for breakfast.
- Project ready; engaged project guru.
- Respects and maintains confidentiality.
- No problems: an anti-party animal and a solid citizen.

YOU HAVE TO HIT THE BULL'S EYE IN EXECUTING YOUR DIRECTIONAL TARGETING

Next, we planned out how Brooke would maneuver interviewers into the Interview Court Hot Spots and leave them without doubt that she was a very good fit for these additional areas.

When planning out your Directional Targeting, design your delivery with fluidity. That is, leave flexibility in your plan.

In the interview, you are going to maneuver interviewers to Interview Court Hot Spots by raising the topic when it fits the flow.

Additionally, do not be afraid to be brave if you need to insert your Directional Targeting Statements into the interview play.

One good opportunity to initiate your Directional Targeting is when you get asked a question related to the Directional Targeting topics. Or if you get asked a general question like the "Tell us about yourself" question, you can utilize this question to maneuver interviewers to Interview Court Hot Spots.

Be prepared to initiate Directional Targeting when you get asked the classic question "Do you have any questions for us?"

Alternatively, you may have to be bold and initiate proactive Directional Targeting when it might not exactly fit.

Next, are some role-plays to exemplify the technique of Directional Targeting utilizing Brooke's internship interview.

Interviewer: Tell us about yourself?

Brooke Hit Back: Personally, or professionally?

Interviewer: Professionally.

Brooke Directional Targeting: Well, I love to write. I am really detail-orientated in my writing and reviewing. I have just always loved writing. I also thrive with project work. I have a great track record with delivering projects.

Brooke Hit Back: Tell me, do you expect completion of a project as part of this internship?

Interviewer: Yes, we do, and you get to choose the topic of your project.

Brooke Double Punch Prep Statement: That is fantastic. I have a project in mind.

First Punch: I thought it would be advantageous to the firm to be able to analyze the financial impact on clients for cases that meet certain criteria.

Second Punch: I believe with some mentorship I could make such a project successful and provide valuable data to the firm.

Interviewer: Thank you for the clarification; that is very helpful, and writing skills are very important to us.

Brooke Directional Targeting: Oh, great. Can I also add that I am an independent worker and do not require a lot of micromanagement? I get things done. I also thrive with project work.

Brooke Hit Back: Are my skills in being an independent worker and managing project work important to you and to the position?

Interviewer: Yes, absolutely, we value those skills and abilities very highly.

Brooke Double Punch Prep Statement: That is great. I feel I am a really strong fit with your culture and business needs.

First Punch: I have a strong track record in working independently and delivering results.

Second Punch: I also thrive in managing projects from conception to finalization. I have always ensured projects deliver top results and that they are on time and on budget.

At this point in her interview Brooke had successfully hit home three Directional Targeting Statements, each reaching Interview Court Hot Spots, and she believed she had gained additional Big T Factor points as a result.

But at this point in her interview, it did not fit to pursue the other two remaining Interview Court Hot Spots: good citizenship and confidentiality.

Brooke waited for another opportunity in the interview to win these Interview Court Hot Spots—when the interviewer asked the "Any questions for us?" question.

In the next role-play, Brooke initiates Directional Targeting to capitalize on gaining the Big T Factor.

Interviewer: In concluding the interview today, we wanted to thank you for your time.

Brooke Hit Back: I have really enjoyed it. Before you close the interview, can I take a moment and share some insight about me that I think is pertinent to the position?

Interviewer: Yes, of course.

Brooke Directional Targeting: I want to reinforce my absolute position on maintaining confidentiality. I take confidentiality very seriously and have never had an issue in breaching customer or client confidences.

Brooke Hit Back: I just wanted to confirm if that is important to you?

Interviewer: Oh, yes, of course. We have very strict standards in maintaining client confidentiality.

Brooke Double Punch Prep Statement: I expected such a standard and want you to know that I am fully aligned to keep that standard.

First Punch: I would never breach client confidentiality.

Second Punch: I will with absolute assurance uphold your standards of conduct in that regard in and out of the office.

Interviewer: Thank you; we appreciate you sharing that with us. Our standards of conduct are very important to us, and we take any breaches very seriously.

Brooke Directional Targeting: Conduct is also very important to me. I fully understand that I would be representing the firm twenty-four seven. I take that obligation very seriously. Therefore, I would be very careful to maintain professional behavior.

Brooke then Hit Back to determine the interviewers' feelings regarding this Interview Court Hot Spot of representing the firm twenty-four seven and sealed the deal with a Double Punch.

In my experience, Directional Targeting is crucial to gain incremental Big T Factor points.

With limited interview time and core job criteria to cover, there will only be so many questions in the question lineup.

Usually, the interview question lineup will not cover everything that is important to the employer.

I believe you need every extra rating to get the job, and therefore you should take the initiative to get to Interview Court Hot Spots and win bonus Big T Factor points.

From the Directional Targeting role-plays, you can see that the technique combines effectively with Hit Backs, Double Punch Prep Statements, and Double Punches to produce a powerful quadruple combination.

Plan to execute your Directional Targeting with precision to cover three to five Interview Court Hot Spots in each job interview.

Gain every edge you can in your interview to **get that job**. Strive to gain every extra Big T Factor rating point from interviewers.

Directional Targeting is designed to assist you to do exactly that to win every incremental point.

Ultimately, Directional Targeting enables you to Interview Strong.

CHAPTER SEVEN

ARMOR UP WITH STRATEGY

When candidates get that prized job interview, as their job coach I ask them, "What is your interview strategy and plan?"

They usually respond:

- "What are you talking about?"
- "I don't have one."
- "My strategy is to panic."

I often reiterate, "What is your strategy and plan for the interview?"

If you consider the amount of work required to get an interview, don't you think it is worth the effort to prepare an interview strategy and plan?

On average, it has taken a month of hard work, if not longer, for you to get this interview. It has likely taken multiple applications and several tough networking initiatives. After all that hard work and effort, you finally have an interview, which is gold!

Are you really going to walk into that interview room without a strategy and plan?

My daughter Zoe is talented in art and animation. But it is a competitive industry to find work in for a college student. After some networking efforts, she learned the college art school had a potential opportunity for a model. Her networking inside efforts eventually secured an interview to be an art model.

Wow! Think about that for a moment.

No networking, no job.

She was excited to have this opportunity. Her interview was coming up, and I was observing her preparations. I ventured a question.

"Zoe, what is your strategy and plan for the interview?"

I could tell by her reaction that she had not considered a strategic interview plan.

She was excited about the interview, all right. She had planned out what to wear, down to the type and color of her shoes. But she had no actual interview strategy or plan. I am not being critical; in her status of preparation, Zoe was on par with most college students who have an upcoming interview.

*To significantly increase her chances of
getting the job, Zoe would need to work
on an interview strategy and plan.*

We worked together and identified core job criteria for the art model position and designed Hit Backs and Double Punches to address the criteria. We also designed Directional Targeting Statements for Interview Court Hot Spots that would be highly valued by management.

Then we preempted Tough Questions and role-played how to turn difficult questions into Big T Factor points.

Finally, what about closing the interview? We designed some Closeouts for her. I address Tough Questions and Closing Out interviews in upcoming chapters.

*We then captured all of these techniques
in an interview strategy and plan.*

Zoe executed her interview strategy brilliantly working through her plan, Hitting Back to get behind questions, Double Punching to increase the Big T Factor, and maneuvering the interviewer to several key Interview Court Hot Spots on the interview court.

Some of those Tough Questions also came her way, and she was ready to handle them and turn them into Big T Factor points.

Long story short, Zoe got the job. I believe it would have been virtually impossible for Zoe to achieve all the *Interview*

Strong techniques and skills and win the job without a well thought through strategy and plan for her interview.

> *I do not think you can achieve*
> *professional play like that on the fly.*

It is much like being a professional golfer. I understand that the top professional golfers, after checking in to their hotel for a golf tournament, get out and go to work. Their priority is not to stay in the hotel and enjoy the spa. No way—you do not win like that.

The top players, the winners, get out of the hotel and go to work. They walk the golf course. As they walk, they observe the lay of the land, speed of the greens, position of the bunkers, location of the trees, and where the water traps are. In their mind they go through each shot.

Can you imagine being a professional golfer and securing a place in the U.S. Masters Tournament, and then going into the tournament without a strategy or plan for your game?

> *Imagine the consequences of getting that*
> *job because you took the time to design a*
> *strategy and plan. Life-changing, right?*

Winning that job can change your life. A job can determine where you live, the car you drive, how you spend your time each day, what kind of contribution you can make, your opportunities for development, and the ability to make other choices in life.

Given the impact a job has on your life,
I believe it is essential to go into a job
interview with a strategy and plan.

DESIGNING YOUR INTERVIEW STRATEGY

The *Interview Strong* Strategy Template will assist you in identifying and establishing an interview strategy and plan. The template has a waterfall approach, a natural flow from the initial identification of core job criteria down to designing your Hit Backs, Hit Back Chasers, Double Punches, and Directional Targeting.

The template will then guide you to capture your closing statements and ultimately summarize your interview strategy into a plan.

Once you have your strategy captured in a plan, you can go over the plan and practice it to prepare for your interview.

I have observed that candidates are far less nervous when they interview with a practiced strategy and plan.

Reducing your nervousness is worth everything.
I have also observed that candidates who pay the
price to complete a strategy and plan feel empowered
and are more interview ready than those who do not.

I have actually seen the confidence level of candidates skyrocket when they have completed and memorized their interview strategy and plan.

It is so amazing for me to hear the report after an interview on how a candidate executed their plan. I hear sound bites like:

"It was so awesome when I nailed my first Double Punch. The impact was highly effective."

"My Directional Targeting really paid off. You could see them nodding in agreement."

"My Hit Backs completely changed the interview. I was able to get behind most of the core questions and really sell myself."

"I am usually really nervous, Mark, but this time I felt different. I felt empowered and ready."

"The Interview was challenging, and at first I did not know what to do. Then I recalled my plan and Hit Back and Double Punched my way out."

"I totally forgot to Hit Back the first question on a core job criterion. Then I remembered to do a Hit Back Chaser."

"I was so glad I was ready for Tough Questions. They asked me my greatest weakness, and I turned that question into a Big T Factor win."

"They asked me what my salary expectation was, but I followed the Let's Talk Money principles in my plan, and it turned out to be a great discussion."

"Per my plan, my mindset was to approach the interview in Date Mentality. I did not interview in Test Mentality, nor did I Interview Assumptively. The interview was so different as a result. It was a discussion."

"I was struggling with my unemployment. Soul Essentials and Soul Tactics were in my plan to review and internalize. They have really changed how I feel and how I view myself. I am interviewing more confidently."

The *Interview Strong* Strategy Template has a waterfall flow design that commences with job criteria from the job posting and flows down through key steps, all resulting in a plan.

The following is an outline of the steps in the Interview Strong Strategy Template.

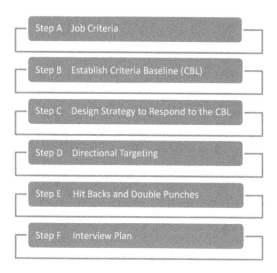

INTERVIEW STRONG STRATEGY TEMPLATE

STEP A. JOB CRITERIA

List the core job criteria listed in the job posting.

1.	2.	3.	4.	5.	6.	7.	8.

STEP B. ESTABLISH CRITERIA BASELINE (CBL)

Condense job criteria down to five to seven main topics. What the employer is really looking for. This is the Criteria Baseline (CBL).

1.

2.

3.

4.

5.

STEP C. DESIGN STRATEGY TO RESPOND TO THE CBL

Define your strategy statements to address the CBL.

1.

2.

3.

STEP D. DIRECTIONAL TARGETING

Create your Interview Court Hot Spot Statements.

1.

2.

3.

STEP E. HIT BACKS AND DOUBLE PUNCHES		
Identify Hit Backs and Hit Back Chasers. [Reference the core job criteria in Step A and strategy statements in Step C]	Identify Double Punches. [Reference the core job criteria in Step A and strategy statements in Step C]	
1.	1.	2.
2.	1.	2.
3.	1.	2.
4.	1.	2.
5.	1.	2.
STEP F. INTERVIEW PLAN Summarize strategy, Directional Targeting, Hit Backs and Double Punches into an interview plan.		
1.		
2.		
3.		
Etc.		

The following is a completed example of the *Interview Strong* Strategy Template for an interview strategy and plan for an IT account executive position. To simplify, I have only included five job criteria.

To commence step A, start by listing the core job criteria from the job posting.

Moving to step B, condense down the job criteria into a criteria baseline (CBL), which should be articulated in statements that capture what the employer is really looking for.

INTERVIEW STRONG STRATEGY TEMPLATE
STEP B. ESTABLISH CRITERIA BASELINE (CBL)
Condense job criteria down to five to seven main topic statements—what the employer is really looking for. This is the Criteria Baseline (CBL).
1. Seasoned account manager.
2. Strong talent to close sales and build relationships.
3. Solid and experienced territory management.
4. Top presenter at executive level.
Note: You will usually be condensing from eight to ten job criteria down to say five to seven statements. Remember I am providing an example using five criteria being condensed down to four statements.

These statements should capture the essence of the job in several statements. Examples of this step would be condensing down the job criteria to statements such as: "Executive management acumen," "Deliver sales results," "Cut costs," "Manage the team," "Deliver projects on time," and "Budget, design IT solutions."

In the following example I condense the five job criteria down to four baseline statements.

- Executive management acumen.
- Deliver sales results.
- Present cost savings and solutions.
- Manage the team and deliver projects.

Now moving to step C, build your interview strategy to respond to each CBL statement. Strategy statements could be like the following:

- Ensure the employer understands I am seasoned in account management and can deliver sales results.
- Show cost cutting examples, demonstrate project management skills, show executive management acumen as well as presentation skills.

These strategy statements are the foundation for your interview plan.

INTERVIEW STRONG STRATEGY TEMPLATE
STEP C. DESIGN STRATEGY TO RESPOND TO CBL
Define strategy statements to address the CBL
1. Need to clearly communicate that I am a seasoned account manager, a guru, not a novice. need to talk years and showcase some points to reinforce this point.
2. Show I am a top closer (detail stats) and talented in building relationships (need some examples here for talking points).
3. I need to be clear in demonstrating I can present at the executive level and detail examples of success.
4. Ensure I am clear on my certifications – achieved and/or in progress.

Once you have your strategy statements written as shown previously, complete step D, which is to formulate your Directional Targeting Statements.

INTERVIEW STRONG STRATEGY TEMPLATE
STEP D. DIRECTIONAL TARGETING
Create Interview Court Hot Spot Statements
1. *Punctuality: This is something you do not know about me and it is not on my resume, and it is something I believe is important to you but has not been discussed today; I am known for my punctuality. I always arrive ten minutes early to every appointment; That is my standard approach to business.*
2. *Honesty with clients:* ...
3. *Impeccable dress and presentation:* ...

Once your strategy and Directional Targeting Statements are finalized (as in the previous example), you can complete step E, add more content to your strategy by drafting Hit Backs and Double Punches. To draft your Hit Backs and Double Punches effectively, I recommend you reference your strategy statements (in step C) and the job criteria (in step A).

In this example, Hit Backs could include a Hit Back on account management, sales closing, presenting at the executive level, and certifications. To support each Hit Back, Double Punches should also be planned that state your two strongest selling points and respond to each job criteria.

You cannot totally plan your Double Punches because will have to deliver these in the moment, as you receive clarifying information from your Hit Backs.

However, I believe it is good practice to have your Double Punches planned the best you can in order to identify your two strongest selling points for each job criteria. This will help you deliver customized Double Punches in the moment.

For this example, I include some specific examples for Hit Backs and Double Punches that I formulated from referencing the job criteria in step A and strategy statements in step C.

INTERVIEW STRONG STRATEGY TEMPLATE		
JOB CRITERIA AND STRATEGY STATEMENTS SHOULD BE REFERENCED		
STEP E. HIT BACKS AND DOUBLE PUNCHES		
Reference the core job criteria	Identify Hit Backs and Hit Back Chasers	Identify Double Punches
Account Management	1. I hold over ten years seasoned experience in account management. Does that level of experience meet your needs for this position? OR What are you really looking for in your account managers?	Prep Statement: Account management is my passion. 1. I hold over ten plus years' experience and I have refined my skills and approach. 2. I know I will be a strong addition to your team and a high fit to your culture

In the previous example, to design my Hit Backs and Double Punches for the job criterion of account experience, I reviewed the job posting criteria and my strategy statement for account management.

I can now move on to the next job criterion, closing sales, and then the next criterion and so forth, following the same process.

Spending time planning out your Hit Backs and Double Punches is essential to being able to deliver Hit Backs and Double Punches in the interview moment.

It might give you some comfort to know that the first time I attempted to execute my interview strategy and plan in a real interview, my mind went blank, and I started to interview in Test Mentality and to Interview Assumptively.

As I sat there, I thought, "What am I doing?"

I regained my composure, pictured my plan in my mind, and started to follow the plan like a road map.

All of sudden I had a sense of control and empowerment. It felt like I found solid ground for my feet to stand on. I delivered my first Hit Back, and the interviewer responded and provided additional information. I then Double Punched, and it felt awesome. Then there was a pause as the interviewer was madly taking notes. Then I delivered a Directional Targeting Statement.

INTERVIEW STRONG STRATEGY TEMPLATE		
JOB CRITERIA AND STRATEGY STATEMENTS SHOULD BE REFERENCED		
STEP E. HIT BACKS AND DOUBLE PUNCHES (CONT.)		
Closing Sales	2. What kind of closing ratios are you looking for in this position? OR What is most important to you regarding closing ratios?	Prep Statement: My past record speaks for itself with a higher closing ratio than what you are seeking. 1. I am at an eighty percent close in the last ten months. 2. I also close without any fake promises or false gimmicks. I am totally aligned to your standard of integrity.
Relationship Building	3. What do you value the most in relationship building with customers? OR In building relationships with customers, what does your culture value the most?	Prep Statement: 1. I also value building relationships based on true principles. 2. I do not just build relationships but lead them to results. I believe therefore I would be a high fit to your culture

INTERVIEW STRONG STRATEGY TEMPLATE		
JOB CRITERIA AND STRATEGY STATEMENTS SHOULD BE REFERENCED		
STEP E. HIT BACKS AND DOUBLE PUNCHES (CONT.)		
Certifications	4. You sighted certifications in the posting, can I ask what are the main certifications you require?	Prep Statement: Thanks again for the further information. 1. I hold all the certifications you require. 2. I also just commenced a refresher course last week to ensure I stay current
Presentation Skills	5. Regarding presentation skills, what is the most important skill you are looking for? OR What do you value the most in client presentations?	Prep Statement: I am known for being efficient and concise. 1. I have over eight years' experience designing board level presentations. 2. I also have a proven track record in enabling good discussions that lead to decisions

Following my interview strategy and plan completely changed my interview. It was so awesome to practice out the *Interview Strong* technique and skills. I never went back to my old way of interviewing after that experience.

To finalize all your good strategy work, I recommend that you frame all the strategy content into an interview plan so that you can reference it in preparation for your interview.

Therefore, in step F on the template, go ahead and capture the strategy, *Interview Strong* techniques, closing statements, and other important points into an interview plan.

Your interview plan should include several focus points upfront to help you. Focus points are personal and customized points for you to concentrate on to give you every chance for success. Examples of focus points are:

- Do not interview in Test Mentality, and do not Interview Assumptively.
- Go through Soul Essentials prior to interviewing.
- Remember Emotional Adaption in regard to the level of seniority for this position.
- Learn the Let's Talk Money principles and apply them when discussing salary.
- Review the chapter on Tough Questions

Next, the template has sections for you to capture and summarize Hit Backs and Double Punches for each job criterion, Directional Targeting Statements, and a Closeout. (I will cover closing statements in a later chapter.)

The interview plan should be concise, so it is easy to remember on notes in your phone or on several pocket-sized cards.

Remember my first experience in utilizing a plan? The fact that I had my plan to visually remember, and recall was a great help to me. Having the ability to go over your plan again and again prior to interviewing, will enable you to recall and follow it in the interview moment.

Covering your focus points prior to the interview will also help you. Including points of emphasis just for you in your plan is like doing important stretching for targeted muscles before commencing a marathon race. Your focus points can be just what the doctor ordered to prevent any interview injuries.

I recommend you memorize your plan and assign each point of your plan to fingers on your hand. In the interview, you can keep track of your plan by touching each finger very casually. Whatever works to keep you on track will be effective and far better than having no plan.

STEP F. INTERVIEW PLAN

Summarize your strategy, Directional Targeting, Hit Backs and Double Punches into an interview plan.

1. Focus Points—Do **not** interview in Test Mentality—**stay in Date Mentality—Emotional Adaption—Be ready and willing to adapt prior.**

2. Hit Backs—
   Account Management
   What are you really looking for in your account managers?

   Closing
   What kind of closing ratios are you looking for in this position?

   Relationship Building
   What do you value the most in relationship building with customers?

   Certifications
   You sighted certifications in the posting, can I ask what are the main certifications you require?

   Presentation Skills
   Regarding presentation skills, what is the most important skill you are looking for?

3. Double Punches
   Account Management
   List your Double Punches for each core job criteria. This is just good preparation. The strongest Double Punches are delivered in the moment in response to the insight and additional information derived from interviewers from your Hit Backs.

4. Directional Targeting
   Punctuality: This is something you do not know about me and it is not on my resume, but is something I believe is important to you, but we have not discussed today. I am known for my punctuality; I always arrive ten minutes early to every appointment. That is my standard business approach.

   List all your Directional Targeting Statements – usually up to three to five statements to address three to five Interview Court Hot Spot areas is most effective.

5. Closing Statement – I will cover closing statements in an upcoming chapter

Of course, not every interview will go according to your plan, but preparing a strategy and plan and having a road map, even though you may have to adjust, is far better than having no preparation, no road map, and no plan. I understand that if you are nervous when interviewing or if you are new to the *Interview Strong* technique, your process will not be perfect, especially at first.

You may forget the plan slightly in the interview moment, or you may only remember or utilize a percentage of your strategy and plan. That is okay. It is better than nothing. But over time, with practice, I believe you can become very effective in using an interview strategy and plan.

You will likely hold multiple jobs in your career and have to interview more than once, therefore *Interviewing Strong* is a technique worthwhile cultivating.

In my experience, those who take the time to develop a strategy and plan and execute it in the interview become very strong interviewers. They have a greater chance to think clearly, articulate more accurately, gain higher ratings, and have a premium chance to increase the Big T Factor and to ultimately *Interview Strong*.

EXECUTING YOUR INTERVIEW STRATEGY AND PLAN

I am applying for a job posting for a senior account executive at a large competing corporation in the IT solutions market. I want the job. My research shows that I am compatible with company culture. I meet nearly eighty percent of the job criteria. I networked inside to determine what the employer is really looking for.

I knew one of the account executives, and we had lunch. I found out that the previous incumbent drove them all nuts by not coordinating pipeline sales with production requirements. The incumbent was amazing at closing sales and account growth, but everyone hated him on the production floor because every week customer orders were a surprise and often required overtime. The lack of coordination was hurting the production bottom line. Meanwhile, the incumbent drove away in a red sports car with a sales bonus.

I have also practiced having the right mindset and approach in order to interview in Date Mentality. I have prepared my mindset to not follow the traditional process and therefore not to Interview Assumptively.

I have finalized my interview strategy and plan with Hit Backs and Double Punches. I have worked hard to plan Directional Targeting for bonus points. I have also planned out a Closeout to end the interview. My first goal is to build a high level of the Big T Factor and progress to the final three candidates.

The interview is with Mary, the regional sales director, and Carl, the human resources manager. Mary commences the interview with a question.

"Tell us about yourself?"

I think about my interview strategy and plan. This question is not significant to my Hit Back and Double Punch strategy. However, I could use this question to maneuver to an Interview Court Hot Spot to deliver a strong Directional Targeting hit. I learned that the reason why people want to come on board is a big deal in the company culturally. They hold a high preference for people who want to come on board to have passion for their products as opposed to coming onboard just for compensation. I hit the first question back.

I respond, "Personally or professionally?" This gives me a few seconds to think.

Mary says, "Oh, well, we have reviewed your resume and feel like we know you professionally, so share something about yourself."

Again, this question is a good opportunity for me to hit home my first Directional Targeting Statement.

I respond, "Thank you. I am passionate about the IT solutions industry, and I have wanted to come to your firm for a while now, as I have always been impressed with your products and your leadership in the market. I am actually passionate about your products. It is not all about compensation for me; it is more about the opportunity to work at your company and advance your product range. That is my primary factor in applying."

I decide to continue on with a quick Hit Back. "Can I ask, does my motivation in applying fit your culture?"

Mary responds, "Yes, absolutely. We highly value candidate intent and motivation in applying." I deliver a Double Punch to seal the deal on my motivation and intent in applying.

This conversation is going well. I will continue to stick to my strategy and plan.

Mary continues with another question. "Tell us about your closing skills."

Per my strategy and plan, this question is a big deal. It was identified and included in my job criteria baseline and captured in one of my strategies. This question requires me to get to the root of it to be sure that I fully demonstrate my selling abilities, but more importantly, it allows me to connect with what is most important to the employer. This question requires a Hit Back to achieve my strategy and to really understand the business drivers.

For this question, I have Hit Backs and Double Punches ready in my interview plan. I practiced until these were second nature to me. I am cool and savvy as I execute my plan—well not really!

Nerves get the better of me. Before I know it, I am running off at the mouth. I realize that I dived in fully to answer the question in the traditional process. I told them all kinds of things about my closing sales skills. But then I start to remember the techniques from *Interview Strong,* and I realize I am Interviewing Assumptively. I do not even know if my answer was pertinent to what they are looking for. I need to recover.

I execute a Hit Back Chaser to ensure I get a high Big T Factor on this question.

Hit Back Chaser: I want to make sure I completely answer your question about closing. I have a lot of skills and experience in closing. Can I ask, what are you really looking for in closing skills?

Interviewer: We are looking for someone who can close at extremely high ratios. We also want closing of sales achieved with no false promises. We have had some trouble with that in the past.

Double Punch Prep Statement: Oh, I am so sorry to hear that you have had trouble with false statements. I would never do that. I would like to let you know that:

First Punch: I love to sell, and I deliver beyond my sales targets consistently. I close over seventy percent of my accounts.

Second Punch: I hold certifications in closing, and I always strive for account satisfaction and high service. I have never had a complaint regarding my ethics.

Mary and Carl are madly taking notes, but I want to ensure I really hit the target with further Directional Targeting and finish with a Double Punch. I want a Big T Factor for this job criterion.

Directional Targeting Statement: I would never make false statements to customers. That kind of behavior always comes back to bite you. I won several integrity awards for high customer service and transparency.

Hit Back: Can I ask, does my approach, sales record, and closing rate meet what you are looking for?

Interviewer: Absolutely. Your integrity, passion, and sales performance are a high fit for us. We also ensure through regular audits that our account executives have represented us professionally and meet our standards of conduct. Your closing rate is high.

Further Hit Back: That is great. What does your ideal account executive look like?

Interviewer: [Provides an oral profile of the ideal standard, which includes an emphasis on team collaboration.]

Double Punch Prep Statement: Thanks, Mary. As I listen to your ideal account manager profile, I am a very high fit. I would like to tell you why I think that:

First Punch: I have a proven track record of over ten years of consistently passing my targets, and one of the keys to achieving that is not only client relationships but also coordinating with production.

Second Punch: I have also trained more than twenty team members over the years, and I am passionate about building team capability. If you hire me, I will not only meet your ideal profile but surpass it, including in sales, production coordination, and team building.

Note how the Hit Backs in this example were highly effective. The *Interview Strong* technique helped me gain the additional background information driving the question, such as the employer's concerns about false statements and the need for audit compliance. The Hit Back regarding the ideal profile also provided information on the emphasis on team collaboration, which was previously unknown.

Both of my Hit Backs enabled me to use Double Punches to seal the deal on closing sales and team training, based on information which I likely never would have known if I did not Hit Back and had responded to the interview question per the traditional process.

The Double Punch, therefore, was effective in this example, and the corresponding ratings and trust level I achieved should be higher as a result.

I was also able to address the issue of integrity with a maneuver to that Interview Court Hot Spot and deliver a solid Directional Targeting hit.

The next question is a standard one regarding how I build relationships with clients. I hit this question back, as it is sales-related and meets my strategy and plan to do so. I need to get behind this question to ensure I build the Big T Factor.

I can say with confidence, "I am client-focused. I build relationships with clients."

Now time for a **Hit Back:** "Can I ask, what is your philosophy for building client relationships?"

Mary and Carl talk at length about the ABC methodology that they teach and train to their account management. My Hit Back on client relationships has paid off.

Time for a **Double Punch**.

I deliver my **Double Punch Prep Statement** first and then two speedy **Double Punches**: "I am well versed in the ABC methodology. In fact, I have trained several recruits in it." I continue, "The best part of this methodology is to understand business needs. I like to spend time achieving that understanding." I Hit Back further, "Do you allow time for getting inside the business to understand business needs?"

Carl answers, "Oh, yes, we are passionate about achievement in understanding client business needs and allow twenty-five percent of weekly time for exactly that."

Time for a **Double Punch Prep Statement**: That is excellent.

First Punch: I love getting to know business needs, and my track record shows that when I do, I achieve incremental sales.

Second Punch: I also have over five years of demonstrated successful results in understanding business needs and selling in customized solutions.

The next question interviewers ask is regarding administration and reporting. Remember, not all questions require a Hit Back. This job criterion is not part of my strategy or plan, and it would be best to simply answer. There are likely not significant, missing, or unknown gems behind this question. I simply respond that I am highly competent in completing my reports and pride myself in meeting all of my administrational accountabilities accurately and on time.

The interview is going extremely well. It is so empowering to shift the interview away from the traditional process to a discussion —to Date Mentality. I am not Interviewing Assumptively. It is shifting the power to a better balance. I am also using Directional Targeting effectively to gain bonus Big T Factor points.

I have several more Directional Targeting Statements from my strategy and plan to deliver, such as team management, project management, and executive presence, so that I can hit additional Interview Court Hot Spots.

I am about thirty percent into the interview of an anticipated twelve questions. There will be questions that I will simply answer without any Hit Backs.

However, I am waiting for five questions that are core to the job criteria. These questions I will Hit Back.

Overall, I will be very competitive and should be increasing my Big T Factor and ratings more than the majority of competing candidates.

I also have Hit Backs planned and ready to get additional Big T Factor points when they ask the final "Any questions for us?" question. I am not going to use that question for housekeeping—no way. I have some Hit Backs planned: "What does success look like at the company?" and "After getting to know me, would I be a good fit?" I will also use this last question to deliver another Directional Targeting Statement.

I have an awesome Closeout in my plan as well to try to seal the entire deal.

With the support of my strategy and plan, I am *Interviewing Strong* and am on my way to **getting that job**.

RESUME DESIGN

A resume can minimize you or bring out the best in you. I prefer that it does the latter.

CHAPTER EIGHT

A TICKET TO INTERVIEW OR A RIDE TO THE SHREDDER

A pile of one hundred resumes is on my desk. I need to shortlist them down to twelve candidates. I pick up the first resume and glance through education and years of experience. I am quickly reviewing to see if the candidate meets the job criteria and minimum qualifications. It is challenging from the resume format to determine if this candidate meets the criteria, so I move on to the next resume.

From your resume, I need to determine if you meet the job criteria and minimum qualifications.

If you do, I review further to justify advancement.

The next resume is customized to the job. I can quickly see that this candidate meets the criteria. I can also see that they have additional achievements. I advance them to the next round for selection.

I am looking for the top talent. I am looking for candidates who not only meet the qualifications and job criteria but who go beyond the bar in their performance and achievements. I am also looking for a high fit to company culture.

YOU HAVE SIXTY SECONDS

I take approximately sixty seconds to initially review each resume. With one hundred resumes, I cannot on average take more time than that for the first cut. That is the reality. Depending on the job and the number of candidates, your resume is reviewed for approximately sixty seconds. That is right. Think about it. If you had a pile of one hundred resumes on your desk, how much time are you going to give to each resume? I take sixty seconds to decide which candidates advance for an interview or are moved to the shredder. That is why your resume needs to be:

- Content-ready for search engine keyword pick up.
- Designed for quick reference to enable reviewers to promptly see if you meet the job criteria and qualifications.
- Easy on the eye so that reviewers can see your achievements, results, and performance.
- Simple to review in under sixty seconds.

If search engines cannot find key words specified in the selection criteria for the job, your resume will likely not be selected in an online application process.

If a manual reviewer must hunt out key selection criteria or read long paragraphs to find the needle in the haystack, your resume is not on target and will be shredded.

Remember, your resume should be search engine ready, enable quick reference, be simple to read and understand, and easy on the eyes so that the employer can quickly find key content.

WHAT IS A RESUME?

Without fail, I receive mixed responses to this question. Many people do not really understand the purpose of a resume. Here it is:

The sole purpose of a resume is to *gain selection for an interview.*

> *Your resume is a customized key that unlocks the door to an interview and sells you in to do the job. Many resumes read like a profile and do not really sell the candidate in for the job.*

With an understanding of what I have just outlined, you will hopefully view your resume as a living document, a shaped key to open doors to interviews. You will discern the need to customize your resume for the job and do all you can to have your resume updated and aligned to satisfy the job criteria for each application.

When you understand your resume is a key to unlock the door for an interview, you will write and format your resume very differently.

A standard resume will generally not unlock doors to interviews.

IT IS NOT DONE

One of the biggest mistakes I have seen throughout the years is that candidates think their resume is done.

In my experience, your resume is never done.

I believe the approach that your resume is completed is a big mistake. This rationale usually looks like using a one-and-done standard resume to apply to different positions repeatedly. That is the lazy, dysfunctional way.

If you do not customize your resume for each job application, I believe your chances of selection for an interview drop significantly.

If you have multiple skillsets, you should have several versions of your resume in order to apply for jobs in differing industries.

Remember, your resume is never done; it is a living, breathing, fluid document, customized for each job application and updated according to your progression and achievements.

PRESENT YOUR BEST SELF

Make sure your resume does all it can to sell you in and showcase everything you have accomplished and achieved. Your resume should:

- Detail every experience you have gained that is pertinent to the job.
- Demonstrate *every* result that is relevant to the job.
  Many resumes are a profile rather than a powerful facilitator to sell you in to do the job.

Review your resume and change it from a profile frame to a targeted content frame in order to sell you, the best product on the planet.

THE YOU MATRIX: IT WILL SURPRISE YOU

To help you find authentic and strong content to draft in your resume, I have developed a tool I refer to as the You Matrix. This tool is designed to help you fish out from your life and career the key skills, experiences, and achievements that can be utilized in your resume.

The You Matrix is a personal content builder for your customized job applications. Many people often stare at the job criteria in a job posting and think, "I don't have that experience," or, "I don't think I can meet all of the job criteria," or, "I meet most of the criteria, but I don't have anything for that one criterion."

If you do not meet the majority of criteria, then maybe it is better to move on down the road to another job. But what if you meet most of the criteria and are short on some? In that case, you need to strengthen your resume to ensure you get an interview.

Many candidates sell themselves short and do not have the capacity to x-ray their experiences and identify skills that could meet job criteria.

I give candidates a helping hand by having them go to a whiteboard, get a piece of paper or get on their laptop, and complete the You Matrix.

In my experience, the You Matrix exercise helps out most candidates.

The following explanation is an example of how to complete the You Matrix.

- On the top axis of the You Matrix, input each job criterion per the job posting.
- On the side axis, input all of your life and career experience, achievements, and skills.
- For each section of experience, reference the job criteria and match skills, experiences, and accomplishments from your life that fit each job criterion.

This exercise yields additional results for most job candidates. Unless you have already categorized every aspect of your life, you will tend to find at least three to five additional skills and experiences you had not previously identified.

Then you can use these new gems to strengthen your resume for the specific job you are applying to.

Often candidates make the mistake of assuming their relevant experience is limited to past employment only.

However, experience gained in past employment history may only meet sixty to seventy percent of the job criteria. This creates a skill and experience gap.

The You Matrix exercise can help candidates identify other skills and experiences from their lives that can be used to close skill and experience gaps.

The You Matrix covers everything in life; it presents everything you have to offer and every skill and experience you can bring to the table. It is not limited to the narrow focus of your last job.

May I introduce you to fictitious Skye. She graduated from college three years ago in business with an emphasis on marketing. She picked up an internship that led to her first full-time job as a junior account executive. Now she is frustrated, having grown beyond her current role, and needs to earn more money.

Skye's current employer is a smaller-sized organization, and there is limited opportunity to advance. Skye gained a lot of experience from her current job role and also by obtaining several marketing certifications. She has also sat on a collaboration government committee to foster community ad campaigns.

Skye also volunteers at her local sports club and designed and deployed their website. Additionally, she gives guest-lectures once a month at college via her alumni group.

Several recent networking lunches have opened the door to a new opportunity for Skye. There is a posting at a larger, competing firm for a more advanced position leading a small marketing team.

Skye was asked to send in her resume and has just reviewed the job posting. Now she needs help to meet all of the job criteria.

In a moment of despair, Skye thought about declining the offer to apply. The criteria bar appeared too high.

But in this moment, Skye needs to really dig deep into her life to meet the bar for this new job opportunity. She needs to really advance her career and get out from her current position or she will languish there for several more years.

Opportunities like this do not come along every day for Skye, so she needs to really stretch to make this application successful.

Skye needs to look across all aspects of her life, both professionally and personally, to find experience that will satisfy and meet the core job criteria for this position. She has much more solid content built from her life's achievements than what she realizes.

At this point, many candidates sell themselves short, give up, and do not apply for the job.

I have seen candidates miss opportunities when it could have been otherwise.

If they had only completed the You Matrix, the outcome could have been very different for their career movement.

To me, the Skye's of this world deserve every opportunity to advance in their careers.

I want to help every Skye in this world to not miss out on opportunities when it could have been otherwise.

The *Interview Strong* methodology is designed to help you seize those opportunities and succeed.

The You Matrix can assist the Skye's of this world to step out and step up.

Maybe Skye will not find new content for her resume through a You Matrix exercise—but maybe she will! To me, it is worth it to Skye to go through the You Matrix and make sure she is including on her resume everything she has previously achieved in her life. I want to make sure for Skye that she is not missing any past experience relevant to a job criterion.

In the end, Skye utilized the You Matrix exercise. Her You Matrix follows next.

YOU MATRIX	JOB CRITERION 1 Execution of Marketing and Social Media Strategy	JOB CRITERION 2 Experience in leading teams	JOB CRITERION 3 Strong analytical skills in addressing client data
CORE JOB WORK EXPERIENCE (i.e., standard day-to-day responsibilities and duties)	Yes—current job role over three years—included all social media platforms—three major achievements identified.	Not in core job role	Yes—project ABC—need to strengthen it with backup.
SUPPLEMENTAL WORK EXPERIENCE (e.g. stretch assignments, committee member, cross-team projects)	Yes—additional experience with advancing the local government drive safe campaign	Yes—member of local government committee—led a sub-team for social media awareness. *Wow, I thought I had a big gap until the You Matrix helped me match leading a sub-team to meet the criteria	Nothing else here

EDUCATION, CERTIFICATIONS, & TRAINING	Yes—degree majored in marketing. Strengthened with certification in XYZ. *Note: I need to add to resumé	Not really, although I led several team projects as part of my undergraduate degree. *Note: I will identify these and add to my resumé to strengthen the application.	Yes— coursework specific to data. Completed social media data analysis certification course. Wow, I have a third—I did a project as part of my internship that generated a data analysis report.
ADDITIONAL EXPERIENCE (e.g. community involvement, hobbies, life experience	Launched a marketing initiative for the sports club that increased game attendance by 30%	Yes—I did lead a small team of volunteers in designing the website for the sports club.	Gave guest lecture on how to use metadata to drive online sales.

In the previous example, Skye uses the You Matrix exercise to identify skills and experiences that she can utilize in her resume for this job application. Even though Skye has solid experience in meeting the first job criterion, execution of marketing and social media, the You Matrix helped to identify additional experience to really strengthen her resume for this criterion.

Further, Skye initially thought she had a significant gap for the criterion of leading teams, but through the lens of the You Matrix she identified some additional experience from her work on the government committee and her volunteer work for the sports club. Her resume can reference this experience in leading teams, strengthening her application.

The criterion of meeting data analytics is a big deal for this position. Previously, Skye felt she was lacking in this criterion. She had some data analytics experience from her current job—just not enough to meet the bar. But through the You Matrix lens, Skye was able to mine out experience in data analytics from her college years and from guest lecturing.

In this scenario, I only used three job criteria. In reality, there would be around seven to ten job criteria for a job posting. That is when the value of the You Matrix is really magnified.

In the example of Skye's job posting, there likely would have been a job criterion on conflict resolution. Without a tool like the You Matrix, Skye would probably struggle to satisfy this criterion.

However, through the lens of the You Matrix, when Skye analyzed her total life experience, she found gold nuggets for conflict resolution to put in her resume and to reference in her interview.

The You Matrix can indeed surprise you.

The You Matrix can really help you identify past experiences and skills that you previously overlooked and that you can utilize on your resume and later in your interview. Try the You Matrix—it will surprise you.

STRONG RESUMES

To unlock the door to an interview, you need a strong resume. The following is an example of a strong resume design. This design can help you to customize your resume and to quickly demonstrate that you meet job criteria. There are many different resume designs. I like any resume design that aligns to the principles I have previously outlined.

The Two-Page Resume

This resume design I prefer is a two-page template. In this design, you take key job criteria from the job posting and include it in the center of the front page of your resume. In this center section, you can outline and sell yourself, your skills, and experience for the posted job criteria. This is not only great for search engine pick up, but also quickly shows reviewers how you meet the job criteria.

To enable quick reference, other key data about you such as educational, certifications, and achievements are listed on the front page in the left-hand column.

At the top center of the front page are two or three introductory, punchy paragraphs that capture you at a glance. These introductory paragraphs should not be written as a profile but rather customized to sell you in for the job.

The entire front page of the resume is therefore directly selling you for the job and demonstrating why the employer should hire you. I love this approach. To me, this is a strong resume.

Note the power of the *third-person language* of this type of resume.

Resumes drafted in the third person build an element of trust in the reader. Talk about increasing your Big T Factor right from the beginning!

For example, if I write "I am great with animals," the first-person tense of the language is just fine. But when it is written in the third person— "Mark is amazing with animals"—this adds some persuasion because it reads as a third-party validation. This can increase reader trust.

A short, second page is added to this resume to summarize job history and achievements. For your job history, I advise to go back to just your last three jobs with year benchmarks.

Some candidates do not like multiple page resumes, and I respect that. If that is the case, I have also provided a one-page version of this resume design concept. You can also shorten the first page of the two-page resume design and add a work history section at the bottom of the first page, eliminating the need for a second page.

In the two-page resume, the first page is so comprehensive that reviewers can reference the second page, which includes work history, if they desire more detail.

In this example, the quick reference column on the left showcases key educational and other achievements.

At the top center of the front page are two or three introductory, punchy paragraphs that give quick insight into who you are and what you offer for **this job**. These introductory paragraphs should be customized for each application to sell you for the job, and they should not be drafted or framed as a profile.

As previously stated, the heart of the front page is key. This center section mirrors the job criteria from the job posting and should reference your powerful selling points for each criterion. This section, framed against job criteria, is your opportunity to show why you should get the job.

A second page can follow with a brief outline of your past job history and achievements for each job. Remember, I usually only recommend going back to your last three jobs unless there is a job in your history pertinent to the position. An example of this second page of the resume follows next for your reference.

RESUME

Jane Doe
Janedoe@gmail.com
Ph: 310-765-4321

MBA—Accounting
University of ...

Bachelor of Science in Finance
University of ...

Certifications
Cybersecurity
Project Management
Agile Methodology

Top Achievements
Received award
for ...
Designed
consolidations for
ABC corporation
Implemented
security framework
for ABC corporation

Other Key
Experience
Global rollout of ...

EXECUTIVE BIO AT A GLANCE

Jane Doe is a senior financial consultant for corporate information technology systems, specializing in financial ERP systems design, configuration, testing, and implementation roll out. Jane is also experienced in providing client training and support including customizing training material.

Jane is a highly accomplished individual holding excellent education and experience in both finance and information technology systems.

Jane holds professional consulting experience with a diversity of clients, including large multinational corporations.

CORE EDUCATION, EXPERIENCE AND SKILLS FOR [NAME OF POSITION]

For each of the key job criterion, identify the education, experience and skills that meet the requirement and qualify you for the position.

Financial Systems Consultancy Experience: With twelve years' experience, Jane provides clients with best business practice solutions for banking, financial procedures, tax, organizational structures, and legal compliance.

Systems Consultancy Trainer: Jane holds five years' specialized experience providing training to consultants and customizing training material to meet specific corporate needs.

Implementation Project Experience: Successfully implemented Peoplesoft systems across all project phases. Directly involved as senior consultant in assessing business processes and writing detailed specification documents for customized system programming.

Application/Software Savvy: Jane is expert with Peoplesoft, and design integrations to other applications, specializing in finance and banking modules.

International Experience: Completed two global projects meeting corporate and auditing requirements from different countries. Experienced in identifying country-specific requirements.

Change Management: Solid experience in assisting clients with change management issues associated with technology implementations.

Security: Jane is certified in Cybersecurity and has successfully designed and implemented security frameworks to meet core industry standards

CAREER SNAPSHOT	1999–2005	**Senior Consultant** **ABC Consulting Firm** Responsibilities included senior lead on projects over a team of consultants, designing IT solutions, customizing training of ERP systems, and managing client relationships. **Personal Client List:** · ABC · ABCD · ABCDE
		Achievements · Presented to the ABC Executive Board of Directors on finance strategies. · Created training courses for ABC system both for staff training and virtual training. · Worked directly with legal counsel to achieve legal application solutions for business operations. · Duplicate above design for each job that you wish to include.

One-Page Resume Design Concept

Next is the one-page resume, designed under the same concepts highlighted in the two-page resume design.

Space for content is more challenging with one-page resumes, so you need to be really concise without losing your major selling points.

A one-page resume needs to be punchy and straight to the point. I recommend not reducing font size to fit it all in. Small font can make a reviewer's job extremely difficult.

JOHN DOE

M: 310-123 4567 EMAIL: JDOE@....................

EXECUTIVE SUMMARY RESUME

Education

MBA ABC College: Graduated 2016
Bachelor of Science ABC University: Graduated 2012

Account Executive Bio

John is an exceptional and highly experienced account manager. John holds over eight years' experience in managing account growth, driving sales, and managing teams. John possesses extensive experience in delivering customized client solutions, sound judgment in handling difficult client issues and is immaculate in his planning. John is known as an "closer" and "achiever". John gets things done. Confident, good demeanor, especially under tight deadlines, with an eye for detail, John delivers results.

Awards and Achievements

ABC.
ABC.

Professional Experience and Skills for Position ABC

Awesome Account Manager:
John is a proactive account manager, arranger, planner, and builder of account portfolios.

Super Sales Executive
John improves sales performance and hits targets, reduces inefficiencies, and drives growth. John eliminates account issues that hinder expansion and builds relationships.

Closer and Growth Guru:
John is a closer. John delivers results. John's engagement with clients is amazing. No matter how difficult the situation, he manages it to a resolution. John is respectful and timely.

Presentation Skills:
John is a top presenter. Skilled in holding attention and creating focus. John is seasoned in delivering to senior executive management, and to all audience needs.

Experience		
ABC *Present* Account Manager	*ABC* *2016* Sales Manager – Northern Region	*ABC* *2012* Sales Representative

THE YOU MATRIX AND YOUR NEW RESUME

As I was finishing this book, I had the opportunity to work with a wonderful new client, Taylor. She was applying to a job in communications and needed help. Taylor had recently graduated with a great GPA, had solid experience from internships and other initiatives she had pursued through her college years.

Taylor had indeed worked very hard, was very smart, and would be a great employee for any company in her designated field. With great pride, Taylor presented to me her current resume, which she was about to submit for an application to a communications job. I took one look at her resume and said, "No way." I told her not to use it. I explained that this resume was not doing her any justice. She would not be able to build the Big T Factor with this resume. Nor did I see this resume getting her short-listed for interviews.

> At this point, I think she was very deflated
> with my feedback. I was sure she was
> thinking, "What the heck! Mark just rocked
> my resume world. I have been working hard
> on this resume, and now what do I do?"

I reassured Taylor that she simply needed a resume make-over and that she would be very glad she invested the time to rework it. I guaranteed that she would be blown away by the outcome.

Like most college graduates, I could tell Taylor had not been exposed to more strategic and professional resume formats. I believe she had utilized the standard recruitment office resume.

Many students also struggle to fill professional resume designs because such designs have a lot of space for very little content. But I find that the You Matrix exercise can greatly assist students to identify additional content for their resume. Generally, with the You Matrix, students can utilize a professional resume design that they previously thought was beyond their grasp.

Taylor's resume makeover was awesome!

I interviewed Taylor and took her through the You Matrix exercise over the phone. I wanted to mine out from her life the most relevant content in order to meet the job criteria. The following is Taylor's initial resume that she presented to me, with minor edits for privacy.

TAYLOR ABC

M: 123-456 7890 · EMAIL: TAYLORABC@GMAIL.COM

EDUCATION

UNIVERSITY   APRIL 2020
Bachelor of History and Political Science
- GPA 3.73
- **Member:** Women's Honor Society, Feminists, Anti-Human Trafficking Club, Pre-Law
- **Coursework:** Political Parties, Interest Groups, Model United Nations, United States History, U.S. Women's History, U.S. Immigration History, Middle East History, Turkish

PROFESSIONAL EXPERIENCE

Senate Campaign, Intern Organizer   **September 2018-December 2018**
- Coordinated events with organizers and volunteers to address campaign needs
- Composed memos and research about individual policies and campaign strategies for staff
- Established and supervised two phone banks

Museum of Art, Gift Shop Cashier   **April 2018 -Present**
- Managed the duties of a cashier and prioritized other organizational tasks needed
- Strong product knowledge and understanding of target customers

ABC Lobby, Legislative Director   **May 2019-Present**
- Collaborated with State Legislators for meetings and events with their offices
- Wrote curriculum to address subjects such as tax reform and strategized lobbying
- Recruited members and increased the membership rate by 50% within the first year

Research Assistant, Public Relations   **October 2019-Present**
- Researched primary and secondary documents in various locations
- Composed concise and detailed reports on evidence within sources

ABC Company, Student Ambassador   **November 2019-Present**
- Coordinated and hosted sponsored events on campus with a $5,000 budget
- Increased the Student Ambassador membership by 50% within the first year

PUBLICATIONS

Taylor. "ABC". XYZ News

SKILLS

Proficient in Microsoft Office	Detailed research background

AWARDS AND INTERESTS

Model United Nations: Outstanding Delegation	Dean's List - Winter 2020

To me, this resume reads like a personal profile rather than a resume. In my experience, this resume will not effectively build the Big T Factor for Taylor, nor will it show why the employer should hire her for the job. It will also take time for a reviewer to get through the content to determine if Taylor meets the job criteria.

> *Ultimately, this resume does not*
> *sell Taylor in to do the job.*

To produce a new resume, as previously indicated, I took Taylor through the You Matrix session, and we mined out a lot of great new content. I then helped her design a new resume customized for her application to the communications job.

We ended up with an awesome resume that blew Taylor away. I wish I could have videotaped Taylor's face as she witnessed her resume transformation. She lit up and was like a different person and beamed with confidence.

> *A resume is like painting a self-portrait. When you*
> *stand back and observe the portrait, it can either*
> *cause you to beam with confidence or sink in despair.*

I find it such a shame that many candidates just do not have a great resume self-portrait when they could and should.

The following is Taylor's new custom resume. I hope you can see the *significant* differences.

RESUMÉ

Taylor ABC

Taylorabc@gmail.com
Ph: (123)45678910

BACHELOR OF HISTORY AND POLITICAL SCIENCE
ABC University
GPA: 3.73

DEAN'S LIST 2020

POLITICAL SCIENCE
Writing Advisor for the Social Sciences Lab.

OXFORD UNIVERSITY
Lecture Series on religious freedom.

ULSTER UNIVERSITY
Lecture Series on conflict and implications of tribalism in Northern Ireland.

MEMO DRAFTING
Drafted memos for non-profit organization and campaign.

INTERN CAMPAIGN ORGANIZER
Coordinated events, composed memos and research for policies and strategies, established and supervised phone banks.

MODEL UNITED NATIONS TEAM
- National Conference NY
- Awarded Outstanding Delegation

BIO AT A GLANCE

Taylor is a professional collegiate graduate, passionate about her work in communications. Taylor is talented in communications work with over two years' experience in the communications field. Taylor is also uniquely experienced in possessing copyediting skills. Taylor holds demonstrated experience in writing engaging press releases and was published in a major state news outlet.

Taylor will apply to law school for 2022 intake in pursuit of a career in social justice and human rights.

Taylor participated in a semester abroad, studying International Human Rights in England, the Netherlands, France, Switzerland, and Ireland.

Taylor is seasoned in social media, including creating content pertinent to the audience and maintaining relevance.

Core Education, Experience and Skills for Communications Manager Position Posted on _____ job number _____

- **Education**: Excelling in achievement, Taylor graduated early and made the Dean's list in 2020. Taylor brings a depth of writing to engage readership.
- **Communications Experience**: Taylor has for the past two years fulfilled communications deliverables across several projects, customers, and industries.
- **Copyediting Skills**: Taylor has consistently demonstrated her copyrighting skills and abilities.
- **Self-starter/Contributor in team environment**: Taylor has consistently demonstrated her self-starting and contributing abilities in a team environment.
- **Social Media Management**: Taylor holds a proven track record in the media space for special interest organizations.
- **Project Management**: Taylor has a strong record of delivering projects on time and meeting all deadlines.
- **Experience with Publishing Software**: Taylor is experienced and fully skilled in publishing software

CAREER SNAPSHOT	2018-2019	**U.S. SENATE CAMPAIGN**
		INTERN ORGANIZER **Achievements:** · Established and managed two phone banks. · Worked with entire staff to achieve communication initiatives and frequently managed volunteers. · Wrote an op-ed that was published in a national newspaper.
	2019-2020	ABC COMPANY
		STUDENT AMBASSADOR ABC is a non-profit organization that provides young Americans with reliable information about the economic and fiscal policies, programs, and challenges that will impact their lives. **Achievements:** · Stewardship over budget and hosted events. · Spearheaded communications projects including social media and campus outreach. · Led public relations communications efforts for recruiting and volunteering.
	2019-2020	ABC COMPANY
		LEGISLATIVE DIRECTOR ABC company enables lobby experience during the legislative session and connects them to local civic engagement pipelines. **Achievements:** · Collaborated with State Legislators for meetings and event coordination. · Wrote curriculum to address subjects such as tax reform and strategized lobbying opportunities. · Recruited members and increased the membership rate by 50% within the first year.

What a difference professional resume work makes!

I am so proud of Taylor. Candidates like Taylor will go far in life and in their career because they are courageous and reach out and up.

It is so important to work hard on your resume, to paint your best self-portrait. How vital, to customize your resume for each job application.

Your resume should be in top-notch condition. To achieve that, I recommend that you avoid the following blunders.

TOP RESUME BLUNDERS

In resume screening, I have seen human resource professionals and managers care a great deal—and sometimes even disdain—the following blunders.

Your Objectives

From my experience, I would suggest you do not list your objectives in your resume. I believe that employers do not generally care about your objectives. To me, employers care about who you are, your fit to the job criteria, and if you possess the required skills and experience to achieve *their* objectives.

Employers want to find high-fit and low-risk candidates to interview.

To me, stating your objectives upfront is like starting a date by sitting in your car and, before pulling out of the driveway, telling your date that your objective is to marry them by the end of the night. It is more than off-putting; it simply does not fit.

"I Am a Quick Learner"

To me, this statement is very hard to quantify. It is determined by your self-evaluation and is therefore constructed by your personal bias. This statement usually highlights lack of awareness and inexperience.

Quick learning does not apply to industries or complex jobs that take years of experience to obtain skills in. Throwing the quick learner statement around is like throwing a pebble at a large skyscraper and hoping it has an impact. This statement can also backfire and be perceived as you seeking to cover your skill deficiencies. Rather than if you can learn quickly or not, the employer cares more about if you can do the job, can do it today, and have ready-set-go capability.

"I Have Great Interpersonal Skills"

After years of a career in human resources, I am still not sure what this statement means. Think about it. Does this mean you are a great debater, friend, spy, empathizer, champion, talker, or guru gatherer around the water cooler? Does it mean you possess ability to read peoples' auras? Or are you just a good conversationalist?

I recommend that you not include this statement unless you can quantify it. It is stronger to specify in the communications space certain skills you have.

Skills and Experiences Not Relevant to the Job

I have seen so many resumes over the years that list content, skills, and experiences that are not relevant to the job being applied to. That old career history and achievement may be important to you—you may even be proud of it—but it does not matter to interviewers if it is not relevant to what they are looking for to do the job. If you can, take out irrelevant content, or customize the content the best you can to demonstrate that you can do the job you are applying for.

Multiple-Page Resume

Your resume is not your memoir. Do not make it more than two pages. Unless it is otherwise standard in the industry, including pages and pages will ensure no one will read it.

> **Remember, the purpose of a resume is to open the door to an interview.**

Your Hobbies

I recommend you do not put hobbies in your resume unless they apply to the job. You can speak to personal hobbies in the interview if it fits to build the Big T Factor or if interviewers ask. But generally, do not put your hobbies in your resume. I am talking about hobby statements like this: I like running, fishing, hiking, taking baths, being sporty, hunting, taking in mountain vistas, cooking, having my toes rubbed, shopping, family time, and finally the incredible, awe-capturing unique super strength hobby—I like to read!

You get the point, right? Unless any of these personal hobbies and interests are strongly linked to the job criteria for selection, reviewers do not generally care, and if they do, they can ask you in the interview.

Endlessly Long Cover Letters

Remember, your cover letter needs to be quick, to the point, and concise. Too long and you are gone to the shredder. A cover letter should be no more than three concise paragraphs, perhaps with several direct, powerful bullet points between paragraphs to break up the flow. Bullet points in a cover letter provide a layout that facilitates a quick and easy reference.

Your resume is an extension of you and should reflect the very best "you" it can. Your resume should not be a profile but a facilitator to sell you in for the job. Customized resumes are key to getting interviews.

You should work hard to have an awesome,
inspiring, sell you in, customized resume,
to unlock the door to getting an interview,
so that you can Interview Strong.

INTERVIEW SKILL
AND TECHNIQUE II

Some doors can only be opened by networking.
One needs to master the art of Interview
Rhythm and Winning with Tough Questions
in order to *Interview Strong*.

CHAPTER NINE

NETWORK INSIDE

I was very excited. As a new college student, I had an interview. The job posting was for a part-time office administrator at a ballet school. The hourly pay was good, and the hours fitted my class schedule. I will be honest—I spent more time thinking about what I was going to wear than on researching the company or working on my interview skills. I had an awesome outfit: gray dress pants and an apricot shirt with a gray knit tie. That was the fashion back then. I looked spiffy. My thirty minutes of researching the ballet school had me feeling confident, but I was actually armed, and dangerous!

The interviewer was a professional, very astute lady who managed the ballet school. She was a living symbol of the fine arts—refined, articulate, polite, and sharp. As the interview progressed, it became very evident I was out of my depth.

*"Tell me," she said, placing in front of me a black
and white photograph of a male ballet dancer center
stage, dressed in tights, high in the air, legs far apart
in a perfect split. "What do you see?" she asked.*

I was expecting to be drilled on admin skills, not be asked for my interpretation of a photo. She was going for the jugular. I panicked. I did not know what to look for in the photo or what to say. All I could see in front of me was a dancer in tights, doing the splits. I think I replied, "Flexibility."

I could tell from her reaction that my answer missed the target. There was not going to be a second interview. The photo and I were gracefully discarded.

Truthfully, I had no idea what the ballet school valued. Even though she finalized the interview with some further questions on admin skills, I knew the interview was as good as over.

It was obvious that I did not know what the school culture was, nor did I understand their business and educational strategy nor anything about the school's ballet technique or style.

My lack of preparation communicated that I was a selfish candidate. I was there solely for the money. Not good indicators for a healthy, long-term employment relationship. Would you hire me if you were her?

Several years later as a new college graduate, I sat on my couch pondering my upcoming interview with a world leader in fast-moving consumer goods.

My resume had secured a first-round interview. I had learned what I could about the company, which was very limited. The fear of failure started to hit me when I remembered my ballet school debacle.

I did not want to interview the way I did at the ballet school, and I realized I had to put in more interview preparation to win.

Let me pause this story. If I had this interview today, I would research the management team and try to take one of the team members to lunch. Anybody would do—anyone who would accept my lunch invitation, anyone who I could gain knowledge from. Everyone usually eats lunch. I would start with employees who are closest to the area or function of the job. Anyone inside the company or any employee in the business process or supply chain. Anyone who is working in areas of integration with the company would also be effective for Networking Inside. Think of vendors, customers, suppliers, etc.

Of course, sometimes it is all iron-clad shut tight. I get it. But many times, customers and suppliers are willing to help you. There have been some companies that I have tried to Network Inside with, but the walls are wide and high.

> *But I do not let that stop me. I sketch out*
> *on a pad all the integrations: customers,*
> *vendors, suppliers, and partners.*

Maybe, I could interview one of their customers to understand the company better, and then that meeting may provide some further leads to pursue. Or what about working for free for a day with a supplier, or going on the road with one of the company sales reps, or job shadowing an employee for a day, or visiting with a supplier or customer to better understand business needs?

You need to try to Network Inside. Can you interview a vendor or a competitor? Do you have a friend of a friend?

Some people are really talented with Networking Inside because they have developed the skills and acumen through years of experience.

> *I do not know if anyone ever graduates*
> *from the Network Inside school.*

I am still developing and refining my own Network Inside skills.

> *To do this well—to get inside—takes*
> *masterful networking, time, patience, a*
> *lot of hard work, thought, and the ability*
> *to move through chains of people.*

Let us return to me on my couch as a young college graduate. I had the concept of a Network Inside technique developing in my mind, formulating in its infancy. I could not get inside this company directly; they were like a vault.

I got off the couch, put my suit on, and walked up the street to the largest supermarket in town. The supermarket was after all, a retailer of the company's products.

I determined to interview the supermarket store manager about the company. I was lucky enough to get some time with the store manager, and he taught me about the industry and how a supermarket worked with suppliers. As our visit concluded, he motioned me toward the grocery aisles and indicated that a merchandiser representative from the company I had an interview with was working in the store that day.

This experience taught me that you never know where networking can lead you.

I joined the merchandiser and offered to work by her side for several hours.

The merchandiser was building a food product display at the end of a grocery aisle. It was dirty, hard work. I worked alongside in my suit, on my knees at times, right there on the supermarket floor. But we talked. I asked questions and listened. I learned so much about the company.

I gained insight into what the company valued and how they operated. I learned that some of the company product lines came into the retail store, delivered directly, and other product lines came through the supermarket warehouse, ordered by the supermarket staff against stock levels.

I also gained insight into the merchandising strategies deployed to achieve increased sales. Upon finalizing the job shadow, I had a greater understanding of the business. Before this experience, I would have had to Interview Assumptively. But now I felt like I really had a chance to *Interview Strong*.

Long story short, the merchandiser informed company management about a persistent, hardworking candidate that job shadowed for several hours. They were impressed with my initiative.

I was also able to reference the learning in my interview and demonstrate my newfound knowledge of their products and merchandising strategies.

> *Networking Inside paid off and transformed*
> *my interview into a discussion. I got the job!*

I learned later that I was one of three graduate hires from over one thousand applicants. Think about the odds. Think about the total number of candidates. Over a thousand! There were three jobs. The chances of receiving a job offer were slim.

*I was very naive. The odds of getting that
job were low—nearly insurmountable. I
expected the hire harvest without any work
because I was a big college graduate.*

I was learning that a top job with a leading company is gained under very competitive conditions and that it requires hard preparation work. It would be fair to say that many of the other short-listed candidates had similar education and part-time job experience as I had. It would also be fair to say that many of the other short-listed candidates satisfied job requirements. What gave me the edge?

*I attribute getting that job, my first job
out of college, to the power of heaven and
to the power of Networking Inside!*

With the knowledge gained from Networking Inside I was able to *Interview Strong.* I was also able to facilitate a very different type of interview; I initiated several discussions. I asked questions in the interview that enabled me to understand the real intent of their questions. I was able to adjust and change my responses to gain higher ratings for each interview question.

*Network Inside, helped me to not interview in
Test Mentality, nor to Interview Assumptively.
Do all you can to Network Inside.*

Principles of Networking Inside

- Map the company supply chain and integrations.
- Contact, build relationships, and learn.
- Use relationships, references, names, insight, and learning in your cover letter, resume, and job interview.

WHAT ARE THEY REALLY LOOKING FOR?

Once I applied for a senior global human resources position. The posting listed key criteria based upon the job description. One of the requirements was the "ability to work with stakeholders." I had no problem satisfying this criterion. To prepare, I initiated several Network Inside meetings over lunch.

From Network Inside meetings, I saw a common theme emerging.

Many managers hated the previous incumbent because they all felt like they had been dictated to for years. Managers and peers felt they had products forced upon them—products which did not fully meet the true needs of their customers. Stakeholders felt excluded, ignored, isolated, and disempowered.

What the management team was really looking for was not expressly stated in the job description or the job posting.

When I was interviewed for the position, the issue of exclusion of stakeholders was not clearly articulated in any of the interview questions. The closest question addressing this issue was focused on ability to work with stakeholders. This kind of interview situation is not unusual.

What management was really looking for had not fully translated into interview questions.

Stakeholders wanted early consultation from the commencement of product development, and the posting and job description did not provide any granular detail around this need.

My Network Inside efforts had exposed this crucial information.

I could now align my resume and interview to this deeper aspect of working with stakeholders.

When the "Can you work with stakeholders?" question came up in the interview, I answered with targeted responses. I spoke to my ability to work with stakeholders and to my passionate belief in early inclusion of stakeholders from the product development stage and beyond.

How did other candidates respond to this question?

Once the interview process was concluded, I could discern from feedback received that the other candidates did not answer the question with targeted responses. Most candidates gave general responses like "I can always work with stakeholders." But what did an answer like that mean to interviewers? Did it mean that the candidate could manipulate outcomes? Did it mean that the candidate could get their way but politically hold back and nullify complaints? The other competing candidates did not know what management were really looking for. I got the job!

> *Networking Inside helped me to learn*
> *what management was looking for and*
> *empowered me to Interview Strong.*

I have seen the Network Inside technique pay dividends again and again. I always ask those I am coaching to find out what the employer is really looking for and then relate to it in the interview.

> *Network Inside, learn, align, and seal the deal.*

Do you know what the employer is really looking for? Most job postings will be derived from a job description, which is a frame-up of the work, qualifications, skills, and attributes. It is a science.

Sometimes the job description is out of date and historic. Often the job description and associated posting do not reflect the recent office politics swirling around the position.

Many times, office relationships—positive and negative—with the outgoing incumbent play a *significant* role in what the employer is really looking for. This information is rarely factored into the job posting or job description but is at the forefront of the minds of interviewers. Sometimes it is hard coded in the interview questions, and other times it is more allusive.

Find out what the employer is really looking for by Networking Inside.

What do you do with learnings from Networking Inside? Sell yourself against what they are really looking for. Use what you learn from Networking Inside and sell your alignment through your Double Punches. You should also execute your Directional Targeting. Seal the deal. Communicate alignment in your resume, during Network Inside and in the interview.

What are they looking for? Find out and seal your alignment.

BE REALISTIC

I love basketball. There is a high probability that I was a grander basketball player in my mind than I was in reality. I wanted to go pro. It was not until I saw professional basketball players up close that I realized I was not in the same league. Later in life, after years of being absent from the basketball court, I jumped back in like it was the old days. This act provided solid revenue to physical therapists. Two torn calf muscles were the real score.

I asked the physical therapist, "What is the deal with these injuries? I mean, I have been playing all my life."

He responded with a smile and a true reality check. "You are not eighteen anymore, and likely twenty pounds heavier since back then." He had me; I could not argue. The reality check was indeed realistic. Gone were my days of dunking.

To me, the same goes for jobs. Many people want to be a CEO or VP. I am all for helping people achieve their dreams and fulfilling their potential.

But a CEO or VP position is likely not going to happen for you today if you do not currently have the experience, skills, and proven track record for a CEO or a VP position.

I would love to be a professional basketball player, but a professional team is not going to draft me. I could walk on and try out if I could sneak past security, dye my air, lie about my age, falsify my basketball playing history, take medical measures to protect the two torn calf muscles, etc. You get the point. I would not last five minutes.

At one time I thought it would be awesome to be an investment banker, but last time I checked, the bank is not calling me. But my imagination can justify me in applying to investment banking jobs. It goes like this: Yes, I love to bank, I understand investments, I know the difference between a debit and credit, and I have won family Monopoly. I read banking journals and talk the talk over dinner with people in the industry. I am ready to apply! Take me now!

Of course, I have no banking or investment experience, no Master of Finance degree. But wait for the famous line: "I am a quick learner."

I am not a dream killer. I love the candidate who dreams and then goes to work to make that dream happen.

That kind of pursuit requires perseverance and work. The path of becoming an investment banker for me would require going to college at night to get my Master of Finance degree and changing my current job to work in an entry-level position at an investment banking firm. I could apply to more senior jobs over time, especially once I gain my education and build up the required years of experience.

Most jobs have clear requirements and qualifications that are non-negotiable.

Before applying, really understand the job criteria and qualifications, and be realistic.

A solid resume will need to address each job criteria and qualification to increase your chances of getting an interview.

You should really look in the mirror and answer this question honestly: "Do I have what it takes to do the job?" Not only qualifications, experience, and skills, but do you have what it takes to commute or handle the stress of the position, or do you have the gas in your tank to work in the industry and pull the hours required?

Do you really have what it takes to perform and deliver top results? If not, you should move on down the road and apply to compatible jobs. The end goal is to identify jobs that are a high fit to you. Then get to work on a customized resume that aligns with the job posting and prepare your interview skills and techniques so that you can *Interview Strong.*

- Be realistic.
- Do you have what it takes?

CHAPTER TEN

RHYTHM

Have you ever tried to listen to yourself talk for an extended period of time? It is an interesting exercise. Interviewers must listen to you for the length of the interview, typically an hour.

I am going to cover next what I have learned over the years about the Rhythm of personal interview communication. I am going to cover points such as impact Rhythm has on your interview effectiveness, the length of your response time, insight into holding attention with Rhythm, using hands or not, pausing, tone, facial expression, and interaction.

I can meet with a candidate face-to-face and observe and listen to them for around ten minutes and suggest adjustments. Generally, my recommended changes help candidates interview very differently, more effectively than before, with simple adaptions to factors that influence and improve their Rhythm.

I am focusing on your communication Rhythm because I believe it is very impactful to your Big T Factor.

IMPACT OF RHYTHM ON THE BIG T FACTOR

So why am I addressing these communication points? It is not to have you be a communication guru. It is because in my experience, all the hard work you put into interview skills and soul can be derailed with ineffective communication Rhythm, which can reduce your Big T Factor.

Some candidates I have worked with gave tremendous effort on all of the *Interview Strong* techniques and skills and became very skilled in executing their interview strategy and plan.

However, when I sat down with these candidates and interviewed them, they were very—and I mean very, *very*—boring. Their Rhythm of response was too long. These candidates felt more was better when less was actually best for them. In listening to their responses to interview questions, my attention started to fade before they concluded. To make matters worse, their mentality of more was better was impacting their Double Punches.

Their Double Punches were like slow, painful, dull, soft blows.

With this kind of interview Rhythm, these candidates would likely struggle to build the Big T Factor with interviewers.

Think about this very important point.

> *These candidates had invested all the hard work on technique and soul, but their response Rhythm, a vital requirement, could make or break their success.*

It is a solid lesson for all of us that we cannot underestimate the importance of refining our response time and Rhythm.

LONG OR SHORT?

Given that I cannot sit down with you and conduct a Rhythm assessment, I would suggest you get a buddy to work with, someone who can give you direct and honest feedback. The first assessment to conduct on interview Rhythm with a buddy is to determine if your responses are too long or short. Response length time is hard to quantify precisely for each person as it is very individual and because interview questions can vary in the time it takes to answer. When practicing with a buddy, there are some general guidelines to follow.

A response to a question is made up of several sentences or statements. In my experience, each sentence or statement should be around thirty seconds, and collectively, an entire response comprising several sentences should be a maximum of eighty seconds. Some people really fit no more than sixty seconds in their total response time. Others, who have a reflection, pause, and energy in their voice tones, can hit around eighty seconds and be effective.

I believe a full response to an interview question should not be longer than two to three minutes. If you are implementing the *Interview Strong* technique, you will be morphing the interview into a series of discussions. If these discussions are mutual, I do not want to limit the entire discussion time.

To start, I recommend you get with an interview Rhythm buddy and practice your length of response statements. A buddy should be able to provide feedback to you if your responses are too long, boring, or too short. It is a balance.

I have provided three standard interview questions for you to practice answering. In role-plays with a buddy, evaluate the length of your response time.

- Why do you want to work for us?
- Tell us about your experience.
- What are your strengths?

For each question, have a buddy provide an assessment of the length of your responses. Alternatively, you can sit and face a mirror, record yourself, and listen back. Remember, there are usually several response sentences or statements to answer each question with a pause between. I want you to focus on the length of time of each of your response statements. To me, the rule of thumb is thirty seconds for each response statement, with a total maximum in-and-out of eighty seconds. This kind of exercise usually helps candidates refine and understand their communication Rhythm and find improvements.

> *I am looking for refinements to your Rhythm that increase your Big T Factor. Best response time should hold listener attention at an optimal level.*

Cut back your length of response statements if feedback indicates you are too long. Increase response statement time if feedback indicates you are too brief.

HANDS OR NOT?

Using the same buddy or mirror process and the three practice questions provided, I now want to address the use of your hands. Many people utilize their hands to reinforce their communication, especially in interviews.

> *Many people use their hands in an interview more than they do socially.*

My assessment is that many candidates either consciously or subconsciously associate the use of hands in an interview as a nonverbal way of strengthening their verbal communication. Candidates tend to think that using their hands reinforces their answers, makes up for what they may lack, and increases the level of trust.

> *For most candidates, the use of hands distracts interviewers.*

Hands can draw away focus from the face and eyes. This can reduce your Big T Factor.

> **I want interviewers to focus on your face and eyes and really listen to you.**

Such a personal focus on the face and eyes, I believe, can significantly build your Big T Factor.

I do not want interviewers distracted by your hands. When practicing, I usually have candidates sit on their hands to stop the hand aspect from diminishing their Big T Factor.

I advise candidates to hold their hands together in their lap when they interview.

> *They feel like I have cut their hands off, taken away their nuclear arsenal, and removed their secret weapon.*

It would not be fair to dictate a no-hands rule-fits-all policy. There are times when I have recommended that a candidate use their hands in order to provide reinforcement and extra non-verbal strength.

> *Sometimes, hands can make a mouse roar like a lion.*

If a candidate is a mouse in an interview, the use of hands may be well needed. The risk of being a mouse is far greater than the risk of your hands taking away attention from your face and eyes. A buddy can assist you in determining whether you are a mouse or a lion in an interview. That answer will help you decide to what degree you should use your hands.

I always recommend getting an interview buddy to provide a helping hand, excuse the pun. Alternatively, you can sit and face a mirror and assess yourself.

THE POWER OF THE PAUSE

The next component of Rhythm I want to address is the power of the pause. I have seen pausing between response statements or before a Double Punch add power in gaining the Big T Factor. A pause can help you gain interviewer attention.

I can tell you that interviewing candidates for a day makes for a very long day. Candidates who stood out to me were those who utilized *the power of the pause.*

> *That extra pause, that stretch of silence, might just be enough to increase attention.*

Practicing pausing with an interview buddy could make an effective difference in how you respond to questions.

A pause should not be longer than three seconds, but a one- to two-second pause can add some dramatic pause power to responses.

This is especially true just before delivering Double Punches or answering questions that have an element of emotional context, such as why they should hire you, compensation, your weaknesses, willingness to relocate, your greatest strengths, and achievements.

DO THESE AND DIE

There are interview blunders I have noticed over the years that you will want to avoid. There are some major do-nots, such as stalking interviewers and interviewing via video conference with your pets in the background unfettered.

I have included these interview blunders here because I have seen them really minimize the Big T Factor for candidates.

"GREAT QUESTION"

When you are asked an interview question, I recommend you do not classify it or judge it with a response equivalent to something like, "Great question!"

Candidates usually say this because they are nervous and need to gain a few seconds to think.

Instead, Hit Backs provide you time to think more effectively.

You are not there to assess interview questions. I recommend not falling into this trap of evaluating each question, placing a stamp of approval or determination on the question. To me, you are best to pause and follow your interview strategy and plan rather than passing judgment on or making comment about the actual question being asked.

DO NOT ENTER WITHOUT BACKUP

Do not lie or embellish your responses. Good interviewers will hunt down and expose fraudulent representations. Nothing reduces and eliminates the Big T Factor faster than being exposed in an interview.

I have also seen over the years some who miraculously got away with lying through the interview and selection process. However, usually it will become obvious that these candidates cannot perform in the position, or issues are found in later background checks.

"I DO NOT HAVE"

Avoid, if you can, responding to a question regarding a skill or experience by saying, "I do not have." This is hard to do, especially when I emphasize honesty so much and when I just covered Do Not Enter Without Backup.

When you do not have a particular skill or experience, there are several ways in your resume or in your responses to questions to approach "vacant parking spaces."

Firstly, you can be in the process of getting the skill, whatever it is. I try hard to preempt with those I work with, the kind of skills, experience, and certifications the employer will be seeking. I often indicate to a candidate the fact that interviewers will be looking for a certification in project management, for example, so the candidate should register for and get started on it.

*The strategy is that when interviewers ask
for it, you can avoid the "I do not have"
response and instead answer with a "Yes! I am
currently completing that certification."*

Secondly, you can utilize what I refer to as the reference model rather than settling on a blunt "I do not have." The reference model helps you to sight experiences and knowledge you have gained over the years, thus utilizing the little gems you discovered in the You Matrix.

It goes like this. Suppose an interviewer asks, "Do you have experience in project solution management methodology?"

Rather than looking blankly at interviewers and stating, "I do not have," you can utilize the reference model and answer, "Well, I worked side by side with a project manager for eight months who did utilize that methodology. I certainly know it in-depth and can apply it."

A further example: "Do you have experience in leading conflict resolution?" Rather than answering, "I do not have," you can reference a personal gem picked up in the You Matrix. "I sat on a committee that had to manage conflict resolution, so I do have solid understanding of conflict resolution principles."

Notice that the candidate had not led the conflict resolution, but she could reference a learning experience.

A reference is better than nothing—certainly better than "I do not have"—and most of the time will be accepted by interviewers.

Some seasoned interviewers may pursue you to determine the exact distinction between what you have referenced as opposed to what you have done. That is okay; they are doing their job. And if the distinction is vital, I recommend you simply reiterate the reference and show the distinction.

This approach would look something like this:

Interviewer: I want to be clear. Did you lead the conflict resolution process?

Candidate: The committee chair led the process, but I worked very closely at her side for over seven months and gained the experience necessary to lead such a process.

Notice that in this example there was no "I do not have," but the candidate did not lie. Instead, they reinforced the devil in the detail per the reference model approach.

Of course, if you legitimately do not have it and are not in the process of getting it, then you may have to surrender.

Your final attempt can always be to tell interviewers that you will be getting it tomorrow. Just ensure that you can get whatever they are asking you for today, tomorrow.

TALK ABOUT THE WEATHER

I did this once and will never do it again. I was met in the lobby by one of the interviewers. It turned out to be a panel of three interviewers. As we walked through the corridors to the interview room, I was nervous. We were walking in silence. I did not know what to say to build the Big T Factor with the interviewer, so I commented on the weather. As soon as that comment left my mouth, I knew it was the wrong topic and statement. The interviewer was like, "Ah, yeah, it is nice outside." It was clearly awkward. It sounded like I wanted to be outside rather than inside with them.

After that experience, whenever I have been greeted and as we have moved to the interview room, unless spoken to by the interviewer, I lean toward being politely quiet.

This is a time for you to retain your power, not to give it away with silly comments, especially not about the weather. Keep it professional. If the interviewer is chatty on the way, of course you can chat back, but let them lead.

BE LATE AND RUSHED

Do not be late.

Do not be late.

Shall I say it one more time? *Do not be late.*

Be thirty minutes early. That is your new standard arrival time. I will tell you why:

- Interviewers could be ahead of schedule.
- It is polite to be early.
- Being early demonstrates planning.
- Being early demonstrates punctuality.
- Your arrival time will demonstrate to interviewers how you will treat their customers, vendors, and associates.
- Arriving early gives you time to prepare.
- The thirty minutes you gain from being early is time to go through your interview strategy and plan.
- Being early helps you get well-adjusted and helps you get into Date Mentality.
- Early arrival gives you time to breathe and get ready with your Hit Backs and Double Punches.
- The thirty minutes provides time for you to observe surroundings and pick up on clues of what the work culture and environment are like.
- Being early gives you time to remember that you are dating them as much as they are dating you.
- Being early demonstrates your eagerness and your priority for the job.
- You never know what can happen in being early; you might find an additional insight or a Network Inside opportunity.

UN-SHINED SHOES

This is a metaphor for any dress standard that has gone astray, and a candidate brings it all before interviewers' eyes.

My father once told me a story of a candidate who was applying for a pharmaceutical sales representative job. The candidate did a personal pop-in visit to give his resume to the state sales manager. The visit was not more than five minutes—a smart move if you can do it. It was reported that the candidate was dressed immaculately, which was one of the standards the employer valued.

The story goes that the candidate's shoes were so clean and shiny that the manager not only noticed the shoes but was impressed by them. This candidate ultimately got the job. My father joked that this candidate got hired because of his shined shoes!

TELL INTERVIEWERS YOU ARE NOT WORKING

What you are doing currently with your time if you are unemployed is a difficult question to respond to. This question is not a casual question. Employers are not asking you this question for fun.

What people do with their time when unemployed can be an important indicator of their work ethic.

Interviewers will have scanned your resume to determine whether you are currently unemployed or underemployed.

If you get asked what you are doing with your time, the principle is for you to respond that you are busy doing this! You are busily engaged in applying and interviewing. That is the response.

Notice how I reinforced interviewing and applying. If you can, indicate that you are interviewing with several firms in the market and that you are getting close to getting an offer. It is good to be wanted. It is good to show them you are busily engaged and working hard.

> *Do not indicate that you are spending all your days and nights becoming a gaming guru or a beach enthusiast.*

You need to communicate that you are fully engaged in searching for jobs, applying, skilling up and interviewing. It is a full-time job to get a job. That is your job right now, so communicate that, so you can confidently *Interview Strong*.

CHAPTER ELEVEN

WIN WITH TOUGH QUESTIONS

I hate it when that Tough Question comes at you like a freight train out of nowhere. It can be the worst, especially when you are not prepared, and there is no escape. You have to sit there and watch the interviewer size you up, waiting for your response, like a cheetah surveying its next meal, and suddenly, you are the prey.

> *Going into a job interview is like roaming*
> *around the plains of Africa; the chances are*
> *highly likely that you will encounter some*
> *Tough Questions designed to devour you.*

You can therefore count on voracious questions to be in the lineup. You should expect it and be ready to deal with Tough Questions.

Generally, Tough Questions are self-assessment questions. That is, the question requires you to provide a response based on your own assessment of you. Tough Questions usually broach such topics as your greatest weakness or strength or how you handle pressure, manage multiple deadlines, or react to conflict.

I believe Tough Questions are a test within the interview. For example, interviewers in one way do not care what you think your greatest strength or weakness is.

But interviewers do care a great deal about how you handle the pressure of Tough Questions.

Again, Tough Questions are generally a self-assessment. Interviewers are not usually measuring your responses with dynamic, scientific measurement. So why are they asking Tough Questions? Interviewers ask these kinds of questions, I believe, to see how you handle the pressure of the question and what kind of response you will provide under that pressure.

Remember, the main reason why I believe an employer will hire you is your Big T Factor. To me, Tough Questions are generally aimed at determining the level of trust an employer can bestow upon you. Your response to Tough Questions provides insight into you.

- Will you be balanced in your response?
- Will you be defensive?
- Will you be a total wimp, self-confess, and break down?
- Will you be savvy?

- Will you be prideful?
- Will you boast?
- Will you fight to uphold your perfection?
- Do you have a degree of humility?
- Are you self-aware?

Your responses to Tough Questions provide insight into your character as interviewers try to determine your fit to company culture.

> *Your responses can tell interviewers if you are ready to handle the bully executive of the division or the calculating, insecure manager on the other side of the organizational matrix.*

Hit Back Chasers can really help you ascertain the drivers behind Tough Questions.

In coaching you through Tough Questions, I want to stick to principles. I will provide the principle and then response examples. You should develop your own responses and sound bites rather than memorize these examples. In doing so, your responses will be more genuine and increase your Big T Factor.

Apply the *Interview Strong* techniques.

The trick is to not only nullify Tough Questions but to use Hit Back Chasers and Double Punches to turn Tough Questions around and increase your Big T Factor.

*I do not recommend straight-up Hit Backs
on Tough Questions, as you should give your
best answer first and then clarify it.*

Using Hit Backs upfront on Tough Questions will likely appear as if you are trying to game the question before responding.

YOUR GREATEST WEAKNESS

In citing weaknesses, you may step on a land mine. You may unknowingly profess a weakness that will be rated against you highly and may even be viewed as a red light for getting the job. This is the real danger with this Tough Question. You will also be unable to discern where the land mines are, so you are in grave danger of stepping on a mine when you share something about yourself that will impact your selection.

My advice on this Tough Question is to respond with some weaknesses that will not hold core impact to your performance for the job. Examples include:

- "A messy desk."
- "I can work too hard sometimes."
- "Too much dessert."
- "I don't iron my shirt or blouse; I buy wrinkle-free."

My recommendation is to keep responses light or generic and stay on safe ground. If interviewers still pursue you, respond with a professional weakness that is not core to job performance. Then demonstrate recent efforts to overcome the weakness or talk in detail about how you have already addressed the weakness.

For example, your messy desk weakness is being addressed with a certification in operational desk planning.

Or your greatest weakness has been not leaving enough time for staff one-on-ones. However, following a 360 and completion of the best training course on the planet, you have recently adjusted how you manage one-on-one time.

Alternatively, I advise candidates to select a weakness that is within proximity to the job functions but is not a core criterion for the job. For example, for a position in account management, I could voice that my greatest weakness is understanding capacity production planning integration but that I am currently completing a certification in this area to broaden my knowledge and skills of what the production teams face.

The technique to apply is that your greatest weakness can be kind of lighthearted or hold no significant impact in performing the core elements of the job.

Alternatively, your greatest weakness has already been addressed or is in the process of being addressed and is a weakness in which you are building capability.

If you must acknowledge a professional weakness, do not address a weakness that would be of serious consideration against you.

YOUR GREATEST STRENGTH

Here comes the loaded potato. If you are too strong, you could be perceived as arrogant. If you are not strong enough, you could be perceived as weak. For this Tough Question, I want you to have enough sour cream, chives, and bacon on top to entice an appetite but not too much to overload your potato. I recommend your answers be strong but balanced, as well as targeted, to satisfy a significant job criterion.

For example, if you are interviewing for an IT programmer job and if a major job criterion is cutting code, you should respond to such a question in the following way: "I am not being arrogant," and continue, "but my greatest strength is the ability to cut quality code that meets customer needs. It has always been a natural talent of mine to understand customer needs and deliver results."

Or for a job posting for a graphic designer, your greatest strength could be: "Well, I can always improve, but my greatest strength is my dual ability to deliver awesome designs on time and within budget." I recommend that you hit two targets with one stone.

Answer the Tough Question and
tick off a core job criterion.

You could continue on with a Hit Back Chaser and Double Punch to really seal the deal.

WORKING UNDER PRESSURE

With this Tough Question, interviewers are trying to determine how well you handle pressure from multiple business activities and corresponding deadlines. The principle in responding to a Tough Question like this is to negate it. This Tough Question may come in many forms, but a good example is: "How well do you perform under pressure?" This question usually has a follow-up chaser question that asks you to provide examples or a personal experience to support your answer. That is why I recommend killing it.

Responses should be something like, "I don't ever feel pressured; I just work." Another example response to this question is, "I have no problem with pressure," or, "I do my best work under pressure. It motivates me." Do not give this Tough Question any legs or power.

MANAGING MULTIPLE DEADLINES

I believe that for this Tough Question it is best to avoid a discussion on the topic, as it can be a slippery slope to examining your work practices and can therefore open you up to scrutiny. I recommend positively closing this door. To me, that is the best principle in handling this type of Tough Question. Examples range from: "I just get multiple tasks completed," or "I don't have any problems in managing multiple deadlines; I never have," or "I thrive in managing multiple deadlines. I like the variety," or, "I eat pressure for breakfast—I love it." But what if interviewers continue to pursue you? You should have an example ready to back you up, such as how you manage multiple work projects successfully or work longer hours to deliver on multiple deadlines.

HANDLING CONFLICT

Interviewers asking a Tough Question like this want to determine if you are strong enough to face conflict or, on the flip side, to react to conflict with balance.

If employers are asking this Tough Question, then it is important to the job position.

You need to show that you not only face conflict but that you are also unphased by it and possess skills to manage it in a reasonable effective way to resolution. The first principle is to demonstrate a positive engagement toward conflict. Examples are: "I do not mind conflict," or, "Conflict is inevitable; it's part of business. I have no concerns in facing and dealing with conflict." Further, "I welcome conflict. It's only through it that we can improve." You should also have some backups ready for this Tough Question that demonstrate your ability to face and manage conflict effectively. Continuing on with a Hit Back Chaser and Double Punch will help seal the deal and ensure your response hits the target.

WILLING TO RELOCATE

This is one of those Tough Questions you need to have a predetermined answer for before going into the interview. When I say predetermined, I mean predetermined! I tell candidates whom I coach, "On this question, you cannot flinch. You need to nail it back within ten seconds, without a pause or wide-eyed wonderment or nervousness." You absolutely need to go in prepared on this question. Generally, interviewers are looking for any reservations you may have.

In my experience, a pause or caution can make interviewers nervous and question your commitment. To this question, there is nothing worse than a deer-in-the-headlights response.

Here is what a deer-in-the-headlights response looks like to this Tough Question in an interview. After you proclaim endless commitment to the job and the firm, the potential employer indicates that the job requires relocating to their New York office rather than staying in Palo Alto. You immediately start thinking about packing, changing the kid's schools, moving Smokey the cat from her beloved garden, and, lastly but not least, the impact the move would have on your partner. Meanwhile, the sweat is starting to emerge on your forehead, and time is ticking. You start to ask some vague questions about New York and the package but still have not answered interviewers affirmatively. Several minutes later, you are lost in relocation weeds, and interviewers are starting to think they might be better to go with Skye, who told them in under five seconds, "Sure, when can I start? Anything to get the job done," and that she loved New York.

You need to answer this Tough Question in under ten seconds, to be direct, and to leave no doubt. You can always change your mind later. If your predetermined position on relocation is a yes, then you need to simply respond, "Absolutely. I would love to relocate to New York to obtain the position." If your predetermined position on relocation is a no, then you need to simply tell them no and why. But you should add a follow-up question to confirm if there are any other options, such as working remotely and traveling. If you are not willing to relocate, that is okay, but you may forfeit the job, and you need to be willing to accept that. If relocation is a deal-breaker and you determine not to relocate, then you need to own it and accept it was not the job for you. If it is a green light, then own it, move, and enjoy New York-style pizza and Central Park.

YOUR GREATEST FAILURE

You are playing with fire with this interview question, and you need protective gear and a good insurance policy. This Tough Question or any question like sets you up to reveal your biggest mistake and present it in full color on the big screen in front of interviewers.

Why is this Tough Question being asked? I believe it is twofold.

Firstly, as previously covered, it is an interview within the interview, to see how well you will deal with the pressure of such a question. Secondly, interviewers may genuinely want to see if you have had a failure, and, more importantly, what you did about it.

> *The failure in and of itself provides insight into you. How you managed the failure and learned from it provides a deeper dive into your character and leadership.*

In my experience, the general principle for you is to manage this Tough Question in one of two ways.

You can choose to be vulnerable and showcase a failure. Just remember to *always* demonstrate how you fixed the failure and what you learned from it.

Alternatively, you can shy away from this question by simply stating that you have never had a significant failure due to your amazing, cautious approach to life, and that you always do your homework.

To me, the fork in the road should be driven by which option will provide the greatest Big T Factor. You obviously need to build the highest degree of trust from this question.

I believe the rule of thumb to follow is that for jobs that have inherent high risk, you are better off being vulnerable. That is counterintuitive, I know. But for jobs with high risk, interviewers tend to extend more trust to those who are more open and vulnerable with failures, especially when they sight the development gained from such an occurrence.

For example: "Yes, I once had a failure on a client project in not following up on the quality control step. It created delays and burned me in my client ratings. I delegated the task to the quality control team but did not follow up to ensure its completion. That lesson has always stayed with me, and I have never made that mistake again. I would like to briefly share what I learned from it and what I have changed in my management and process as a result."

After sharing the personal development, you can also deliver a Hit Back Chaser and Double Punch to ensure you gain Big T Factor points.

To me, this kind of approach demonstrates vulnerability, honesty, and integrity, but more importantly, it demonstrates what you learned and what adjustments you made.

With this option, you can show how you will never be burned again, that the hard knocks have given you experience, and that you are a seasoned candidate as a result.

I think the lower the risk inherent in the job, the more you can negate this question with a simple approach like the following: "I have never really had a major failure of significance that would be relevant to the position." You could then continue on with a Hit Back Chaser to determine what kind of failure the employer is worried about regarding the position and Double Punch their concern away.

TOUGH QUESTIONS SUMMED UP

You cannot always be prepared for every Tough Question. Somewhere right now in some part of the world in a tucked-away, private human resources office, professional interviewers are conceiving a new, unique, and very difficult question that will challenge us all in the future.

I hope the principles you have gained from this chapter provide you a solid foundation for how to handle Tough Questions.

The trick is to turn Tough Questions
into Big T Factor points.

Be prepared to quickly adjust, use Hit Back Chasers and Double Punches, and turn Tough Questions into Big T Factor points so that you can indeed *Interview Strong*.

INTERVIEW SKILL
AND TECHNIQUE III

How do I end my interview?
My last interview is all I think about!
I cannot eat or sleep without them!
Should I follow up? Should I call them?
How do I talk about money?
Should I accept the offer?

CHAPTER TWELVE

LET'S TALK MONEY

One challenge I have encountered in coaching job candidates over the years is their lack of ability to talk about money. Many find talking about compensation a taboo topic, even to the point of feeling that a discussion on money would be inappropriate or showcase them as money centered, or money hungry.

Well, I am here to tell you that wanting to talk about compensation does not make you a self-centered, money-hungry capitalist! Last time I checked; the employment relationship offers you compensation in return for your labor. It is no secret to anyone in the interview room that you are going to get a paycheck.

DO NOT BE SHY

Therefore, the first principle is for you to shed any shyness or reservation you may hold in talking about money. Shyness in talking money is like going to a restaurant and enjoying an appetizer and entrée but not being willing to talk about or order dessert.

You need to talk about money, and you should. The key is to do so at the right time and in the right way. But first, you should remove from your mindset any reservation or shyness in talking money. Money is not a taboo topic.

The right way to talk about money starts with your mentality. The trick is to approach the discussion with a mature mindset that grasps the understanding of the employment relationship.

> **Inherent in the employment relationship is compensation. Accept and understand what is already accepted and understood.**

When is the right time to talk about money? Well, not generally in the first interview. As the selection process matures, the opportunities to talk about money grow. It is almost always better to hold off talking money until you are getting closer to an offer. Such an approach with timing on your part indicates discipline, patience, and true professionalism. That does not mean you should not be hitting the heck out of the internet to find out all you can on what the compensation package may be or what the compensation range is for the job. You should also be seeking compensation information through your Network Inside efforts.

On the flip side, sometimes, depending on the job and the industry, you can and should ask upfront, at least at a high level, what the ballpark compensation is in order to ensure your time and investment in the interview process is going to be mutually worthwhile. This is especially effective when the employer is shielding compensation. In such cases, you can ask for exactly that—what their compensation ballpark range is.

THE TRUE CHALLENGE: THE LACK OF TRANSPARENCY

Many job postings do not mention compensation. You can get frustrated with this lack of transparency. Doing research on the internet and networking can generally provide enough data points for you to triangulate the compensation.

Do not worry about not knowing what the compensation is if your research indicates that the employer is in your ballpark.

Why? Because you will find out the compensation details at the right time. If the pay is in the ballpark, I recommend you keep proceeding.

How will you find out the compensation at the right time? Easy—you are going to ask interviewers, and then you are going to have an awesome conversation about money. So, get ready and geared up for talking money.

THE CRUCIAL UNDERSTANDING ABOUT COMPENSATION

Total compensation generally comprises four categories:

- Salary
- Benefits
- Bonuses
- Stock

Salary is your actual base income, and you need to recognize that banks and creditors will primarily evaluate your salary for decision-making on creditworthiness. Financial institutions may not consider your bonuses in their calculations since bonuses are not always guaranteed. Thus, your salary alone will likely impact your eligibility for renting, mortgages, and loans.

Benefits comprise additional compensation components like medical insurance, retirement, parking, and gym memberships. Benefits can be extremely valuable and can sometimes load your compensation package significantly. For example, medical insurance plans can be very costly to you personally, especially if the employer plan has a five-thousand-dollar deductible on the front end. That means that you pay the first five thousand dollars of medical expenses before the plan benefits kick in. But if the medical plan is richer, it may not have a deductible at all and hence could be worth up to five thousand dollars a year to you.

The employer may be matching your 401(k)-retirement contribution very handsomely or just with the bare minimum matching amount. Are there additional retirement benefit plans offered?

Daily parking costs can add up if you are paying for them, not to mention what you will save on that gym membership if the company pays for it.

As you can see, you should scrutinize the benefits being offered before you jump for that additional ten thousand bucks in salary. The salary increase could be quickly eroded by a reduced benefits package.

> *I have seen candidates leave employers with high excitement for an additional ten or fifteen thousand in salary only to find that they are worse off due to a reduction in benefits value.*

Bonuses are exciting and add to your total compensation. Many people can make great income with the achievement of bonuses. But you need to be aware that bonuses are often discretionary and are frequently impacted by division or company performance.

Likewise, stock can make the poor rich and the rich richer. But there are some basics to consider before you get excited about stock. You should not count on stock until you can count the money in the bank. Stock options generally return the best when you are early in the game—when the company is a startup, when it is launching a new initiative, or when it is in high growth and can be bought out. To increase in value, stock needs high potential to grow. Of course, stock can increase in value over time, generally over years, due to overall company performance. Either way, go in with your eyes wide open. Stock can be great but not guaranteed, and value in your bank account is dependent upon many variables.

Regarding salary, many candidates, especially graduates, think they can negotiate their salary to the moon. To me, this is simply not the case.

> *Negotiating whatever salary, you want with potential employers, is generally Hollywood.*

If you are the rare exception to this, then, of course go for it.

> *Most jobs are benchmarked based on market pay data. The majority of companies and industries follow this best business practice.*

Jobs are benchmarked and graded on a salary range based on salary survey market data. A job is therefore graded against an internal employer grading system. For example, a management job is a grade ten, and the associate job is a grade seven. Each job grade has a pay range.

The pay range for a job generally has a minimum salary amount, a starting point on the pay range, a midpoint salary on the range (which is equivalent to the average market), and a maximum salary amount (which is at the top of the range). Benchmarking salary for jobs in the market is a science but also a market and legal safeguard for companies to pay according to these pay ranges.

There are salary fences in place. No matter how much you beg, plead, play games, or reference who you know, the fences cannot be knocked down.

Pay ranges ensure legal compliance and protection for pay equity and pay discrimination.

There is, of course, some room to move within the salary fences within the pay range for a job, but even then, there are generally tolerances set for the pay range for a job, such as years of experience and educational obtainment. For example, a candidate may be able to argue that they hold experience to be paid according to the average market, the midpoint on the range, rather than at the starting minimum.

Alternatively, a candidate may argue that they are more experienced and therefore should be above the average market and be compensated above midpoint on the range. But again, a candidate needs "the lettuce in the bun" to get higher on the range. Generally, getting higher on the range requires years of experience as well as satisfying other compensation criteria.

Some rare variables to this are market forces. Sometimes you might be lucky for the market demand and supply to swing your way and enable you to demand the big bucks and pay data fences might be blown away by the literal hunger of the market. This kind of situation is rare but can occur, especially in new industries and if you possess emerging technology skill sets.

YOU NEED TO KNOW BEFORE YOU GO

Okay, so you are advancing in your interviews. It has been a long road. At this point, I wrestle candidates down to the mat for some serious disciplines around talking money. The first discipline is what I call "You need to know before you go." In my experience, you need to know what salary you are going to accept or reject before discussing money. You also need to be realistic.

> *I do not want you flinching when it comes to making decisions on the salary being offered during an interview. You cannot "um" and "uh."*

To me, you should have already crunched the numbers and come prepared to be decisive. You should walk into final interviews ready to go.

> *You should know what you will accept, what you will not accept, what your counteroffer figure will be, and your reasons to defend it.*

If you are going to reject a salary amount, you need to know your alternative counteroffer number and have solid reasons why you are rejecting the offer. This requires homework and thought on your part before the discussion with your potential employer. I recommend that you sit down at a table with a pad, pen, and calculator and work out some numbers as well as reasons to defend your position on salary amounts.

If you do not prepare, you will likely struggle to talk money in the moment and to provide your rationale to support what you want.

But remember, pay ranges will likely govern the amount of flexibility the employer has.

LET'S FIND OUT

Now that you are ready with your numbers, find out where the employer is. I recommend in advancing interviews that you ask about compensation. The technique is to find out what is being offered but also to try to determine as much information as you can about the pay grade for the job and the associated pay range.

The principles of engagement are as follows.

Prep question: I want to ask about the salary for this position.

Then ask: What is the salary you are offering?

Go deeper: Thank you. To understand the compensation for the job, can I ask, what pay grade is it, and where on the pay range is the salary amount you are offering comparable to the midpoint on the range?

This three-step approach can be exemplified as:

Candidate: Thank you for the further interview today. I have enjoyed our discussion. I wanted to ask, what is the salary being offered?

Interviewer: Given that this is an entry position and due to some budget cuts, we are offering $70,000 plus benefits.

Candidate: Thank you. That is good to know. To better understand the compensation for the job, can you please tell me the pay grade and midpoint salary on the range for the position? Or can you tell me if the salary being offered is below or above the midpoint on the range?

You are asking the *grade* and *midpoint* so that you can ascertain if the $70,000 in this case is low or high on the pay range and if there is room to move. Trying to find out the minimum and maximum points on the range will likely be too complex, so midpoint will suffice.

Interviewer: Well, this is a pay grade 10. That might not mean much to you, but I can tell you that the midpoint on the range is around $85,000.

Now that you have this information, you can advance further in talking money. Any information regarding the salary being offered and the position on the pay range of that amount will help you make your money decisions. Sometimes employers will not share the midpoint value, and that is okay.

If the employer is not willing to share the midpoint salary amount on the range, then you can indicate that you understand and respect their confidentiality. But you can default to simply asking if the salary being offered is below or above the midpoint on the range for the job.

WALK AWAY, ON TARGET, OR FUTURE CONSIDERATION

In this example, the salary being offered is $70,000, which is $15,000 below midpoint. Now that you have crunched the numbers and are armed with your predetermined decisions, it is time to stick to your money line in the sand.

WALK AWAY

In this example, the salary is extremely low for you. Your response in this case is to work a lower amount up higher or to be prepared to walk away.

The principles are:

- **Reinforce the love:** Maintain the Big T Factor.
- **Reject the offer:** Make sure you have professional reasons ready.
- **Indicate why:** List your reasons for the rejection.
- **Give a counteroffer:** Have your amount ready to put forward.

If you do this, you need to truly, absolutely be fully prepared to walk away if they do not increase the compensation.

This is not a game. I repeat, this is not a game.

You must mean it and be willing to leave the job behind. Let us see how this could play out:

Reinforce the love: Oh, I am really disappointed. I was really looking forward to joining the team; it is my dream to join ABC company.

Reject the offer: However, I just cannot accept $70,000. But thank you for the offer.

Indicate why: I just could not make it work financially at $70,000. I also believe with my experience that I would be undercompensated at $70,000. I believe I am qualified to advance up the pay range closer to midpoint due to my years of experience and my education.

Give a counteroffer: Do you have any room to move on the range to get closer to $85,000? I understand midpoint is equal to the average market, and I believe I can meet the requirements to be paid at midpoint.

Interviewer: No. Unfortunately, due to budget cuts and this being an entry position, we cannot increase our offer to $85,000.

Candidate: I understand but thank you for your consideration. Please let me know if anything changes in what you can offer. I would love to come on board if you can stretch closer to $85,000.

Interviewer: I see. Well, let me check with our compensation team. Your request would require approval from our compensation director.

Stand up, be polite, shake hands, smile, offer some sincere pleasantries, and leave. Walk out and walk away. Leave it in their court. They will either hire someone else or, if you are their leading candidate, they may seek approval for the additional dollars. Either way, leave it in their court. Move on to the next job.

Your Reasons Are Imperative

In rejecting an offer, your reasons are crucial. If you make it personal regarding the amount being offered, you have lost the game, and this reaction can burn bridges. You should maintain a level of professionalism and maturity.

Your reasons are best based on professional factors such as the offer being overly low in comparison to the market or inadequate to your level of experience. Or the pay is too low on the range to capture your full engagement.

A personal reason can be mentioned, such as that the compensation being offered would not sustain your budget or that the salary would just not work for you personally.

ON TARGET

In this scenario, a salary of $100,000 is offered, which is on par and is on target for your money line in the sand. Your response in this case is to demonstrate acceptance and manage the conversation to a close.

The principles are:

- **Reinforce the love**: Maintain the Big T Factor.
- **Accept the offer**: Be clear and concise.
- **Indicate why**: List your reasons. They should be professional.
- **Closeout**: Have your Closeout ready.

Let us see how this will play out:

Reinforce the love: I would absolutely love to join the team; it would be my dream to join ABC company.

Accept the offer: I accept your offer of $100,000.

Indicate why: I believe that is fair and equivalent to the market and to my experience.

Closeout: I thank you for your consideration.

Stand up, be polite, shake hands, and smile.

Then end with a **Double Punch Prep Statement and Double Punch**: I really mean it in all sincerity. I want the job, and I will not let you down.

Interviewer: Well, thank you for your time today. We look forward to working with you and will email you the offer in writing.

FUTURE CONSIDERATION

In this example, let us say you are offered $57,000, which is slightly low but doable with your numbers. You really want the job and do not want to lose it due to the offer being slightly under your line in the sand.

In this case, I recommend what I refer to as the commitment dollar dialogue.

The principle is to accept the offer but gain employer commitment to revisit the compensation in the future.

This technique looks like this:

- **Reinforce the love**: Maintain the Big T Factor.
- **Accept the offer**: Be clear and concise.
- **Indicate your challenges and concerns**: Be professional.
- **Gain future consideration and commitment**: Be ready to gain future agreement.

Let us see how this will play out:

- **Reinforce the love**: I would absolutely love to join the team; it would be my dream to join ABC company.
- **Accept the offer**: I will accept $57,000.

Indicate your challenges and concerns: The opportunity is key to me over everything else; however, the pay is slightly lower than I expected, and it will provide some challenges for me.

Gain agreement to future consideration and commitment: With top performance, can we revisit the pay in six to nine months' time to consider an increase?

Most interviewers will have no problem agreeing to this concept. It is not a legally binding contract unless you get it included in your offer letter. Some do, which is awesome, but you are gaining the employer commitment to revisit your pay in the future. In six to nine months, you can remind them of the discussion and revisit your compensation. Or if you get the agreement in writing, you can review it with your manager at the agreed upon time. Ensure your performance will back it up.

When all is said and done regarding compensation, if you have not already done so I recommend that you seek to develop the mentality to openly discuss money without feeling awkward.

Accept such discussions as normal, expected, and part of the employment relationship. Do your homework before determining your money line in the sand and make definite compensation decisions before holding money discussions.

Follow the principles we have discussed, and develop your sound bites, wording, and approach. I want you to win when talking about money, whatever winning may be for you.

I want you to increase your Big T Factor, and to ultimately *Interview Strong.*

CHAPTER THIRTEEN

THE WHAT YOU WEAR FACTOR

Many candidates have not thought deeply about why they dress up for job interviews. Most dress to look their best, which of course is best practice. I get many questions on what to wear for job interviews, so I want to include some helpful tips and insights.

In my coaching world, the question "What should I wear?" generally comes up when a candidate has an interview scheduled. It causes much fuss and rush. Most candidates have not really thought about what they will wear until they get the appointment for an interview. I recommend that you do not get caught like that. If you can, have a new outfit for your next interview ready in the closet. Or have your best outfit dry-cleaned and ready to be worn.

You should be Really Interview Ready,
and that includes being dress ready.

There is a lot of research out there on colors of clothing and what to wear and what not to wear for interviews.

I know that some candidates go to great lengths to determine what to wear, even having personal designers, fashion coaches, and color coordinators. Other available resources are, of course, the internet, retail clothing consultants, or a book or TV show on the topic. I admire this specialization and believe this expertise can really help you to improve your dress for an interview.

Opinions and advice vary. I have heard red ties are best for power. No, wear a blue tie for trust. Wear that killer blue or black business pantsuit instead of the blouse and skirt. Dress for power, not for style. And so on. Whichever way, I would like to cover some principles in this chapter that are supplemental to the insightful fashion and dress coach expertise already out there.

I want to address the personal impact of what you wear when interviewing.

Most candidates think you are simply dressing up to be formal or to present your best self. This is true to a degree, but to me this is not the core reason you dress up for an interview.

What candidates wear has a significant impact on their psychological feeling of confidence and fit.

There is nothing like a new suit to make you feel confident and great, right? I want you feeling that way when you interview.

Dress to fit the culture. Fitting in also affects your confidence. Feeling like you fit in helps you avoid being too tight in the saddle and empowers you to get in the Dating Zone.

I believe what you wear has a significant psychological impact on interviewers. I believe what you wear affects and impacts how well you achieve the Big T Factor.

The Psychological Impact of What You Wear

You do not realize how much what you wear affects your confidence level until you are caught out of company uniform. I know from firsthand experience. I was once several weeks into a new human resources senior role and still in the middle of a relocation. I was living in a hotel situated next to the head office. Many of the company senior executives traveling through would stay at the same hotel, so it was a great networking opportunity to meet and greet in the lobby and in the elevators.

One night, one of the senior executives was staying at the hotel. I was in the middle of doing my washing and was caught in the lobby in my bare feet, tracksuit pants, and a rugby jersey. I wanted to run to the safety of the elevators when a member of the management entourage said, "No, you're fine. Come over here and introduce yourself."

Following that invitation turned out to be a big mistake. The senior executive was in a suit and tie, while I was in track suit pants, a rugby jersey, and bare feet. The meet and greet was awkward, and I left a terrible first impression. My confidence was low because of how I was dressed.

> *I not only felt a loss of confidence,*
> *but I also felt like I did not fit in.*

I was out of uniform, out of step, and out of class. It was terrible.

> *My advice from this and years of experience*
> *with interviews is to dress in order to:*

- **Build your confidence.**
- **Fit.**
- **Increase the Big T Factor with interviewers.**

If the employer's dress standard and culture is a pantsuit, then wear your best pantsuit to the interview. If the culture is a suit and tie, wear your best suit and tie. If the dress standard is jeans and a T-shirt, then wear new jeans and a T-shirt. If the dress standard is overalls and boots, then wear overalls and boots.

> *Either way, I recommend that you dress*
> *for self-confidence and to fit in.*

I believe an increase in fit and confidence will greatly increase your ability to *not* interview in Test Mentality, nor Interview Assumptively; to stay loose in the saddle; to Hit

Back smart; to Double Punch with power; to use Directional Targeting with precision; and ultimately to *Interview Strong*.

THE FIRST INSIGHT INTO YOU

What you wear impacts the Big T Factor with interviewers. Remember the story about the shiny shoes? I have interviewed many candidates over the years, and I know that even though interviewers are looking for the right responses and trying to select the right candidate, we ultimately come back to who we trust the most.

> *Your dress can build significant Big*
> *T Factor with interviewers.*

Why is this the case? What you wear should be the easiest part of the entire selection process in terms of winning interviewer trust and demonstrating your high compatibility to company fit and culture. Dress demonstrates your social awareness in regard to compatibility.

> *You control your dress. You alone manage*
> *it. That is why, I believe, dress holds so*
> *much significance to interviewers.*

Dress is your first personal communication to interviewers about you, your social awareness, and how well you fit. Your type of dress will continue after you are hired and will reflect on those who hired you.

Other than your resume, what you wear is the first insight interviewers have of you, to determine your fit to the company culture.

Yes, dress to impress. But more importantly, dress to build your confidence, dress for high fit, and dress to show interviewers your compatibility with the company. Ultimately, I believe you should dress to gain the Big T Factor so that you can *Interview Strong.*

CHAPTER FOURTEEN

WHAT TO DO AFTER YOUR INTERVIEW

Years ago, I got asked the standard question at the end of an interview: "Any questions for us?" I had nothing prepared for this question. I was dumbfounded and could not think of a single question to ask. After taking a few seconds, I just responded, "No, I can't think of anything." It was certainly an anticlimactic ending to my interview, and I could tell it left a slightly negative impact. I not only looked like a deer in the headlights, but I also came across as not very interested in the opportunity or the company. There the interviewers were, sitting right in front of me and granting me time with them to discuss whatever I wanted, and the best I could come up with was nothing at all!

I know now that this question was an optimal opportunity to build the Big T Factor. It was an opportunity I had missed.

At the end of most interviews, interviewers ask you the famous question, "Any questions for us?" If you have followed the *Interview Strong* methodology, you will have turned the interview into a discussion.

However, with this question, interviewers will be expecting you to ask housekeeping questions you may have about aspects of the job that interest you, such as parking or other terms and conditions regarding the work environment.

I recommend you utilize this time for Directional Targeting Interview Court Hot Spots instead. Why? Because using this time for basic questions would be on par with other candidates.

You need to stand out. Stay in gear to increase your Big T Factor to the very end.

You should be using this time to gain more of the Big T Factor than competing candidates have gained. If you planned up to five Directional Targeting Interview Court Hot Spots, you should have one or two remaining.

You can also utilize this time to build the Big T Factor around more personal content. For example, it can be helpful to get a compass point on you as a candidate from the interviewers.

Use this time to x-ray interviewers about your interview performance and to gain further insight and information about you and their view of your fit to the job.

You can ask questions about upward mobility, opportunities to grow within the company, and career paths. The following are some examples of the types of questions you could ask to engender personal discussion.

- I would like to ask how you would rate me following today's interview?
- After interviewing me, do you feel that I would be a good fit to the company?
- After gaining further insight into me, do you see me being successful in the position if I were offered it?
- What strengths do you believe I would bring to the position, and what weaknesses do you believe will stand against me?
- I am a strong performer. Upon excellent performance in this position, what does my career path look like?
- I really want the job. Do you feel that I have what it takes to be successful at this company?
- What do I need to improve in to be able to come on board?

I would like to add that as you get responses to these questions, it is not too late for Hit Backs and Double Punches, to sell yourself against interviewer responses. It is also not too late to Directional Target Interview Court Hot Spots.

While you are still competing, other candidates are closing up shop on this question.

I recommend that you still do everything to get every bonus point of the Big T Factor. You can and should still sell yourself. You can be strong to the very end. Every incremental higher rating can count toward selection.

CLOSEOUTS

Closing a sale is a phrase and technique commonly used in the sales industry.

> **You are selling the best commodity**
> **known to humankind: you!**

Do you think that kind of amazing product deserves a close? I do. I believe you should never leave a job interview without closing it out. To me, powerful closes need to be honest and sincere in order to gain the Big T Factor.

To help you add to your *Interview Strong* technique, Closeouts, let me take you through some examples.

Close It Out with What You Want

Firstly, you need to know what you want. If you want the job, close it strongly. If you are not sure, then close it moderately. If you do not want the job, close it out with a finale.

Strong Closes

Example 1: End the interview with a triple punch Closeout. Stand up, shake hands, look interviewers right in their eyes, and tell them: "I really want the job, I am sincere on that point, and that if you offer me the job I will not let you down." Then walk out.

Example 2: Before you stand up, look interviewers right in the eye and tell them: "Although I am interviewing for other jobs, I will forfeit other opportunities for this job. I really want this job, and I want to work with you."

Example 3: As you are standing up, pause, look interviewers in the eye, and tell them: "I am sincere when I tell you this is the job for me. I really want the job, I am ready, I know I will succeed in the position."

Moderate Closes

Example 1: End the interview by standing up, shaking hands, look the interviewers right in the eye, and tell them: "I am interested in the job and look forward to learning more about the opportunity."

Example 2: Before you stand up, look interviewers right in the eye and tell them: "Although I am interviewing for other jobs, this job is a solid job for me. But I am unsure at this point and would like to learn more."

Example 3: As you are standing up, pause, look interviewers right in the eye, and tell them: "Listen, I want to join this company, but this job is not right for me. Can we explore other positions you may have now or in the future? I would love to visit more to learn about other opportunities that would fit me better."

Finale Closes

Example 1: End the interview by standing up, shaking hands, looking interviewers right in the eye, and saying: "Thank you so much for your time. I have appreciated it. To be honest, I am just not the right fit for this job, so please focus on other candidates in your selection process."

Example 2: Before you stand up, look interviewers right in the eye and tell them: "Your time is valuable, and I appreciate the opportunity to interview. Nothing ventured, nothing gained. But I do not want to waste your time, and I withdraw my application and wish you well in your search."

Example 3: As you are standing up, pause, look interviewers right in the eye, and tell them: "Listen, I can see that ABC corporation is not for me. Thanks for the chat and insight, though. All the best." Head for the door and exit with a polite step.

THE PSYCHOLOGY OF WAITING

After an interview, most candidates are on edge. The interview is all they can think about. They are expecting an offer tomorrow. That is not a criticism. I totally understand the myopic time warp most candidates are in following an interview, as I have experienced it myself.

When you are unemployed or underemployed, your world becomes urgent. But that urgency does not translate to employer pace and timing. Candidates always talk to me about following up immediately or after several days following their interview, especially after not hearing any response. I understand the angst, but again, most candidates are in their own time zone compared to the employer, and at this point calibration is needed.

How do you calibrate being in a different time zone than the potential employer? Easy—move on.

You need to understand that the employer is also running a business and usually does not have the same urgency you do. You are not the only item on their agenda back at the office. It can often take weeks for the next engagement or interview in a selection process.

I have tried to help candidates adjust and be patient, but generally, the gravity of the myopic time zone is so strong and pulls them back so thoroughly that I have learned it is better to rip the band-aid off. I simply teach the following principle as the best remedy.

MOVE ON

Following a successful interview, I encourage candidates to move on. In my experience, that is the best way to help them cope emotionally and get out of their myopic focus.

*Following what they felt was a positive
interview, most candidates are trapped in
what I call—Interview Love Space.*

Interview Love Space looks like this:

- "The interview was so special."
- "We talked, laughed, and exchanged glances."
- "The way they gazed at me."
- "Their offices, the glass, the marble, the snack bar, the fresh flowers in the lobby."
- "I wonder if they are thinking about me?"
- "What are they doing right now?"
- "Did they like me?"
- "What are they saying about me?"
- "Should I send flowers?"
- "Maybe I should send a note?"
- "Should I stalk them in the office lobby?"
- "If I just follow up, it might get things moving."
- "They are all I think about."
- "I can't sleep; I cannot eat."

*Do not get stuck in Interview Love Space.
It is a deadly space to get trapped in.*

If you are stuck in this space, I recommend leaving the interview behind. Say what? Yes, I said it. Leave the last experience behind and move on to another application. Start getting excited about another job opportunity.

Remember, the interview was a date—nothing more, nothing less. I know, it was a great date! But you never know if the date was simply a polite gesture or if your date was just flirting with you and is already engaged to someone else.

Believe me, if they want another interview
date with you, they will find you.

Applying and job interviewing is a lot like gardening. You are planting little seedlings. Your last positive interview was a successful planting. But it is best not to labor the point and be stuck in the garden, gathered around the little newly planted seedling, on your hands and knees waiting to see if it will sprout forth.

I recommend you do not sit at the farmhouse window all night wondering what the little seedling is doing down there under the soil. It is not effective for you to be wondering if the little seedling likes you or if it is growing in another direction or if it is simply dying.

Stop stalking the little seedling!

You will know if the seedling you planted likes your garden. If it likes you, it will sprout forth, and you will see the little green shoots reaching out to you. Until then, in my experience, I believe you should move on to other areas of the garden to plant more seedlings. If the successful interview you had last week comes back for an additional interview, you can simply prepare for it, go back to that part of the garden, and do all you can to encourage the little seedling to grow and blossom. Until then, you need to move on and keep planting.

I know Move On is counterintuitive, but it is the only healthy, functional way I know to get you unstuck out of Interview Love Space. I believe you must keep moving and not get love stuck.

How do you know when you are stuck in Interview Love Space? I believe it is when you are vested too much emotionally in the last job interview you had:

- You want to follow up with too much urgency and frequency.
- You are not passionate about finding and applying to other jobs.
- You think you have the job when you do not.
- You think you do not have the job when you do.
- You find it hard to go on another interview date.
- You are consumed with the last interview date, and you eat, sleep, and dream about it.
- When the rejection call or letter comes, you are devastated. You collapse on the couch and eat ice cream for a week.

Do not get stuck in Interview Love Space.
It is a deadly space. It was only an interview date.

Move on.
You are just dating.
Keep progressing.
Keep planting.
Keep going until you have a job offer.

Once you have an offer, you can get seriously emotionally invested. Until then, keep moving.

FOLLOW UP

One question I always get from candidates without fail is "When do I follow up, and how do I follow up after an interview?"

I do not think following up will make a significant difference to the outcome of the selection process for the job. I know this is very different from everything you have heard before. I am being brutally honest.

Most candidates find that truth hard to take. Often, they feel if they just phone or email back it may swing the door open. Generally, it will not.

Generally, you are wasting your time in following up.

Following up is like believing that gathering around the little seedling you planted in the garden and breathing on it will be a catalyst to the seedling changing its position or will enable it to grow up toward you.

I believe you are better off putting your energies into planting and dating elsewhere rather than following up. In my experience, if they like you and want you, they will find you for another interview, regardless of whether you followed up or not.

In saying this, I am not totally anti-follow up. I admit, on very rare occasions, following up could make a difference for certain jobs or unique interview situations, such as in the sales industry. Maybe the interviewers are seeking the hungriest sales maniac out of the pool of candidates and wanting to assess that strength by follow-up efforts and initiative.

Again, that would be rare and would only apply to certain jobs. I am indicating that, generally, you are better off putting your time into the next interview opportunity rather than following up when it will not alter the outcome of selection.

However, most candidates feel they want to do all they can to get the job, and I respect that. I have seen some follow-up efforts, on rare occasions, net results.

Therefore, I do not totally negate follow up, but if you are going to follow up, I suggest the following principles and techniques.

EFFECTIVE

I believe it is a good approach to ask interviewers what their timing is for selection and advancement.

*Ask if you can follow up and who might
be the best person to follow up with.*

This provides you with not only a good understanding of their timeline but also a follow-up bridge into the organization via a designated contact.

When you follow up, do not make it all about you, as that is the general myopic approach.

Follow up on how their process is progressing to find the right candidate and how you might assist their selection process any further. Do they need any more information from you? Is there anything else you can provide?

You could also try to Network Inside the organization during the follow-up process by networking and organizing job shadowing days and any other experience you can get with vendors or customers.

As you Network Inside, let your designated contact know about your experiences in your follow-up efforts and conversations. You never know what insight such experiences will provide and where the connections and learning will lead.

Another follow-up approach I have seen is letting the employer know you have interviews with their competitor or another company and that you would like to know if they hold a strong interest in you or if you should move on to other opportunities.

Think outside the box with follow ups.
Be creative and professional.

NONEFFECTIVE

From firsthand experience I can tell you: do not stalk interviewers. I recall one interview for which, upon finalizing the interview and returning to my office, I looked up from my desk to find a bright-eyed and bushy-tailed candidate looming over me. I was shocked. Before I could speak, the candidate took great pride in boasting to me that they had found out where my office was, discovered personal management information, and was ready to showcase these amazing investigative powers in the position, which, by the way, the job did not require.

I would recommend you do not burst into interviewer offices with a thank-you card nor show how detail orientated you are by breaching their privacy. Neither do I think it very wise to go to interviewers' homes or to send rambling, multipage follow-up letters. Do not pop up suddenly at their favorite lunch place for an opportune follow-up discussion, unless you are subtle and nimble enough to pull it off.

In my experience, it is better to go in through the front door, so to speak. Invite those involved in the selection process to lunch for a status check and a follow-up discussion.

If you are going to invest the time and effort in following up, part of honoring the *Interview Strong* brand is to execute follow up efforts in a wise, effective, professional way.

If you are going to follow up, do it with class, so that you can be known to be a candidate that will under all circumstances, to the very end, no matter what, *Interview Strong.*

SOUL ANCHORS I

When enduring employment hard times, we all need to wear the right cognitive and emotional gear to be at our personal best to *Interview Strong*.

CHAPTER FIFTEEN

THERE WERE FIVE

It was an ordinary day with a not-so-ordinary request. A familiar voice crackled through the phone. An acquaintance from the career employment office at a local college was reaching out for help. Following the pleasantries came the problem and the request. Five people had been unemployed for months and were working with employment services at the college with little success. Would I be willing to coach them on their interview skills and help all of them get jobs?

"All five?" I asked.

"Yes."

"All at the same time?" I asked.

"Yes."

Wow, I thought as I digested the challenge.

He asked me the question again. "Will you work with these five and see them all through to jobs?"

Compensation was never discussed, as we both knew this would be straight-up gratuity. I swiveled around in my chair for a minute and weighed the request. I knew five people would take literally hours to fully employ. This would be a significant commitment each week. Additionally, they would have to follow my coaching during the crunch times. The key would be if they could trust me. Would they? They did not know anything about me—my background, my experiences, what I could offer. I would likely be telling them to do different techniques than they were used to. Would they be open and willing? Or would they gravitate to the old, standard interview model and approach?

I remembered my own experience of unemployment. It would have been so awesome to have had access to a personal coach who cared about me and was willing and able to help me during that fiery ordeal—not just help me but relate to me and truly understand what I was going through.

> *That thought—to be to the five in their time of need what I lacked in my time of need—was very motivational to me.*

The caller brought me to the point of response, reiterating the invitation. "Will you help?"

I simply answered, "Yes, I will." Then I gave my commitment. "I will not leave the side of the five until they all have great jobs."

I did not know if the five would accept me, but I was looking forward to meeting them. In one way we had already met. Every night as I brushed my teeth, I realized I already held a personal acquaintance with each of the five. The bathroom mirror reflected each one in me—a younger me in another time and in another place, a place we all casually refer to as unemployment.

Meet-and-greet day came. I walked into the lecture room to meet the five. The room was modern, but the faces of the five portrayed an age-old problem—joblessness. I had a slide deck presentation on the *Interview Strong* methodology ready to help us focus on interview skills and technique.

Following introductions, I commenced the slideshow, but I could tell I was preaching the right content at the wrong time.

New, powerful interview skills and techniques were desperately needed, but I had to pause, adjust, and focus on the reactions and the need emanating in the room. The five did not know it, but soul time needed to come first.

I observed that each of the five were feeling as I had once felt when I had gone through my own sojourn of unemployment. I could discern their respective demeanors and their hurt.

Unemployment really strikes at the heart of your dignity at times, and the five were no exception. I stopped the presentation. It was time to remove thorns from paws. You cannot effectively go out job hunting with a thorn in your paw.

I gathered the five in a circle in the middle of the room. It must have looked like one of those touchy-feely group building activities. They were probably expecting me to direct a trust exercise, like "catch me, I'm falling." But that was the last thing the five needed. Instead, it was imperative to address their feelings about their employment predicament. It was Soul Time.

I took a moment to extend an in-depth introduction of myself. I openly shared insight into my own experience of unemployment. I was fully transparent, honest, and raw. I did not hold back on the details, hurt, rejection, challenges, and hard times.

They needed to know that I *understood.* They needed to know I had once been in their shoes and had successfully come out the other side. It was a poignant moment.

I could tell from their reactions that my transparency meant everything to them. They had someone coaching them who understood and held personal experience of their plight.

I pointed to one of the five, a sensitive looking man with large, brown-rimmed glasses, "Tell me about your experience." His tears started to flow. He spoke about the crucible of time to get a job. This was such an unprecedented experience for him. I gently pushed him to share more. He dug deeper, and out came feelings buried down in his core. He spoke about his emotions of being rejected. He spoke about not feeling valued, and then he hit gold.

Courageously, and with brutal honesty, he finally gave voice to the raw, real core feelings. "Nobody wants me!" he blurted out. "No one wants me!" he repeated, with tears running down his cheeks. There was silence amongst the five in the aftermath of those penetrating words. I asked him to speak more to that feeling of rejection. His emotions poured out, and in that moment, in that room, we were suddenly in a sacred, raw human space. One of the five was commencing the healing and strengthening of his dignity, his soul.

This experience reaffirmed my own experience and belief that without facing and strengthening the soul, many people find it difficult to progress in building interview skills. Unresolved emotions can impact interviewing effectiveness. Many people enduring unemployment need to strengthen soul and skills in parallel.

I reminded the group that a lion cannot hunt effectively with a thorn in its paw. You cannot effectively date if you are still cankered by the old relationship. Soul is everything when you are trying to move forward. I wanted to hear from each of the five and enable them to get any negative and unresolved feelings up and out. Today, it was soul time first before skill time.

After hearing from each of the five, I reviewed the *Interview Strong* methodology. I spoke about the need to learn new interview skills and strategies such as Hit Backs, Double Punches, Directional Targeting, not interviewing in Test Mentality, and avoiding Interviewing Assumptively.

I talked through Soul Essentials and Soul Tactics as being vital Anchors to your Soul, especially when your dignity is being attacked as you deal with the rigors of unemployment.

When the session was complete, all five were excited about the new interview approach and technique. All five had cathartically released feelings buried deep down inside. Each soul had been strengthened.

Of course, more work would be needed to learn and internalize Soul Essentials and Soul Tactics. Maybe they would also work with someone they trusted like a professional counselor for further soul intervention. But for now, the session had been a powerful introduction into the importance of addressing both skills and soul.

We all had gained renewed insight into the deep impact unemployment can have upon us emotionally and the need for such feelings to be faced, addressed, and resolved before being able to progress to *Interview Strong*.

I commenced to coach and train each of the five in the *Interview Strong* methodology. It was an awesome experience. I particularly recall one coaching phone call twenty minutes before one of the five had a lunch interview that ended in securing an offer.

I would practice with each of the five, interviewing and re-interviewing them to refine their skills and technique.

I wanted the five to be ready for anything and to be able to handle every interview scenario.

I will continue the story of the five in a later chapter, where you will be able to read their own words and find out what happened to them in their pursuit of employment. You will be able to learn from them, gain insights, and understand that you are not alone in how you might feel or in the challenges you may be facing.

The Five are ultimately a great example of how to *Interview Strong* and get that job.

CHAPTER SIXTEEN
SOUL ESSENTIALS

The Soul Essentials covered in this chapter and Soul Tactics outlined in chapter seventeen are designed to help guard your soul and strengthen it, as you sojourn through your employment troubles. Soul Essentials and Soul Tactics are designed to be your Soul Anchors to ultimately enable you to *Interview Strong*.

Soul Essentials are intended to strengthen how you think and feel in the face of unemployment. Soul Tactics are devised to help you focus on how you act and react under the adversity of employment challenges.

I hope both Soul Essentials and Soul Tactics will help protect you from soul inhibitors that may detrimentally affect your interviewing performance.

I firmly believe that if you adopt Soul Essentials and Soul Tactics as an internal compass, you will have a higher chance to *Interview Strong*.

I have learned that Soul Essentials are more important than you and I may realize, especially when you are going through unemployment and seeking to put your best foot forward to interview. Unemployment strikes at the heart of your dignity, your soul. I have authored Soul Essentials to help you to be your best self when you interview. Ultimately, I want you to be soul empowered so that you can *Interview Strong*.

UNDERSTAND EMPLOYMENT CALCULUS

My client was caught on a snag. He could not accept the end of his employment, especially after all his years of dedicated service. He was taking the business of business personally.

I said, "Here is the first key. Employment Calculus does not always add up." I had his attention, so I ventured further. "The equation of employment does not always sum up to what we expect." I could tell he was listening, digesting what I was saying.

In my experience, this is the first snag many get caught on—the injustice of when hard work and dedication do not sum up to a job, promotion, or eternal employment.

In saying that, I am not negating the worth of hard work and the general return that comes to those who sacrifice and are diligent. Of course, the return for such efforts is generally a wonderful harvest for your life.

I am talking about the fact that there is no forever total insurance policy protecting our employment or absolutely guaranteeing a dream job upon graduation.

I continued with my client, "The key is to accept that sometimes Employment Calculus just does not add up. Our employment can suddenly and shockingly end, or upon graduating college we may suddenly find ourselves without job offers. The overall reaction and feeling that most people have when this occurs is one of failure. They genuinely feel like a loser.

> *"My first message, therefore, is that*
> *unemployment, reductions, and downsizing*
> *are all included in Employment Calculus."*

My client responded, "What about all my inputs, sacrifices, extra hours, and hard work? Don't they count?"

I tried my best to respond. "I believe they do, but such dedication does not always calculate to that special job for the college graduate or forever employment for you and I. Employment Calculus just does not always add up that way.

> *"It is not a personal failure when employment*
> *does not sum out the way we want. It is just*
> *the nature of Employment Calculus. Possible*
> *negative outcomes are embedded in the math."*

His posture relaxed, and his countenance demonstrated to me that an internal light was turning on—the kind of light that engenders understanding. I could see the personal loser label that had haunted him, starting to fade.

> *Accepting that Employment Calculus*
> *does not always add up helped release*
> *him from the loser status.*

Negative outcomes in Employment Calculus are not always held at bay by how good your college grades are, how hard you have worked, how much time you invested at the office, at the plant, in the lab, or in the garden grounds, what you sacrificed, or even what you have achieved and can continue to achieve.

Employment Calculus does not guarantee a continual return to you, even with your labor and investment. Employment Calculus is not always logical or favorable.

When Employment Calculus sums up
negatively, it does not mean you have failed.

We do not blame or brand ourselves as failures when Employment Calculus does not sum up the way we expect.

When Employment Calculus does not add up for
you, what should you do? How should you react?

It is simple: do not internalize it and brand yourself a loser. Do not personalize it. Move on. Keep fighting and keep striving. Fight to achieve your potential, to reach to your next best job. Reinvent yourself, if needed.

If you and I can understand that Employment Calculus does not always add up, we can move on much more effectively.

Those who cannot accept Employment Calculus have trouble moving on. They get snagged.

Unemployment can impact the rich, wealthy, successful, hardworking, and well-educated employee. Unemployment can burst through the door of the single, the married, the parent, the widow, the widower, the graduate, the soon-to-retire, and the meekest, hard-working employee.

Unemployment is generally the business of business. Driven by market forces, even by forces of nature, unemployment can come to all of us despite how good we are at performing our work.

Over the years, I have worked with those unemployed and underemployed from all walks of life and with varied background and experience. However, there is an unmistakable commonality.

Employment Calculus does not always add up; negative outcomes are embedded in the employment formula.

Those who accept and understand Employment Calculus will progress faster than those who do not.

- Do not internalize the "I am a loser" mentality when Employment Calculus does not add up for you.

- Accept that the loss of your employment was simply a result of Employment Calculus.

- Move forward with full confidence and at an accelerated pace to get another job.

MAINTAIN YOUR DISTINCTION

When we introduce ourselves, we tend to synonymously state our name and what we do for employment. An introduction like this is intriguing. I am sure you have heard it before:

"Hi, my name is… I am a…"

Notice the language, name, and then, "I am a job [or what the person does for employment]." Think about this. It is insightful language. This kind of introduction demonstrates how we define ourselves: by our employment.

When I meet a new client for coaching, I listen very carefully to their introduction. I am looking for language as a first indicator of ability to change. In my experience, the language a person uses to introduce themselves and how they define themselves are very important markers.

I have found those who introduce themselves as "I am a [certain job]" or "I was a [certain job]" will struggle more in employment changes than a person who introduces themselves as "I did a [certain job]" or "I worked as a [certain job]."

Why is this view of how we may define ourselves such a factor in determining our ability to change? I believe it is this: What we do to earn income can become intertwined with our identity. We become our work and our work becomes us.

Our personal identity can be sewed together
with what we do for a job, to the point
that we can no longer find the seam.

Our individuality can be consumed by our professional identity. This is such a subtle but vital division, especially when we lose our job.

Therefore, the next Soul Essential is this: Maintain Your Distinction.

I believe this principle is crucial to accepting change in employment. Occupation is simply work you perform. It is distinct from you. Your job can change. Your job can be removed from you by business factors or even by unforeseen personal limitations such as a change in your health or physical ability. You can be demoted. You can be let go.

Clearly, your job is not you. Your
job is work you perform.

Understanding this valuable insight was so invigorating and empowering to my soul when I was in the crucible of my unemployment.

We need to be sufficiently independent from what we do or did for employment to be able to change jobs when necessary.

I believe Maintaining Your Distinction is vital to helping you emotionally adjust when you lose your job or cannot continue your chosen career.

Internalizing this essential will help you to apply, interview, find another job, change careers, shift income, and ultimately *Interview Strong*.

For me, as soon as the distinction between myself and what I did to earn income distilled upon my soul, it became a strong soul guardian.

> *Maintaining the Distinction strengthened me*
> *to be able accept my changes in employment.*
> *It helped me change my career and freed me*
> *sufficiently enough from diminished worth.*

Of course, I felt emotional after my job loss, but once I internalized Maintain Your Distinction, the hurt of rejection or of loss was not as penetrating, and I was infused with a renewal of dignity, self-esteem, and worth.

To me, the soul-filling emotional leverage was real. I found the Soul Essential of Maintain Your Distinction very insulating against job change and unsuccessful job applications.

> *In Maintaining Your Distinction, you valiantly wave*
> *the flag of the value of your human soul in the face*
> *of job loss, unsuccessful applications, being let go,*
> *laid off, fired, demoted, reduced, and kicked out.*

In Maintaining Your Distinction, you uphold your
soul's intrinsic worth and dignity no matter the
status and circumstances of your employment life.

The true story of Katie, in her own words, is a great illustration of the Soul Essential—Maintaining Your Distinction.

Katie explains, "I was thrilled to be hired as a part-time law clerk in the city's largest law firm. I enthusiastically worked while studying for and passing the notoriously difficult bar exam. I was loyal to the firm and felt could contribute. My interview with the executive board of the firm was the best interview of my life. It was brilliant! To me, I had done the hard yards, and it would all be upward momentum. The next step was to advance to a job great offer. I was so wrong!

"There was a job offer, but due to office politics and a threatened, insecure partner at the firm, I found myself minimized and downgraded. The offer was not great nor on par with industry. I was left to my own devices, without support or client work. I found myself in a sink or swim situation. I was being set up to fail. This situation was very confronting and even started to wear on my self-esteem.

"But I knew I was better than the role I was being boxed into and the way I was being treated. I realized that what I was doing was not who I was. I was more than this!

"So, armed with that distinction, I went to work for about a year, networking and gaining my own clients. Initially I did it to prove my value to the firm. But as I gained success, I realized that I could do far better than stay at a firm where I was not treated well. I realized that the very fact the firm had not valued me was an indication of poor fit, that employment is a two-way relationship, and that I should not try to overcompensate for the firm.

"I kept Maintain Your Distinction in the forefront of my mind and channeled my energies into getting a more senior role at another firm.

"To my surprise, I found there were multiple firms interested in me. It felt amazing to accept a new senior role at another firm and take all my clients with me.

"Today, I am growing a prosperous practice.

"I realized that Maintain Your Distinction can lead you to better places. Every day that I am at my new firm and in my senior role, I am grateful I recognized that I was more than my minimized role and that I allowed myself to reach for my potential. We are indeed distinct from our work. Hold on to that distinction. Realizing this fact enabled me to find my potential and not be boxed in and surrender the most important asset I have—me."

What an awesome true story! In my experience, once the distinction between you and your work is set in your mind and heart, any job loss or rejection that may come in your job arena can be processed in a healthier way. Of course, you may still feel hurt or frustrated when you lose your job or get minimized. Many factors determine such decisions, and our immense value as people is not one of them.

MOVE YOUR MANSION

Here is the issue with unemployment and living under the consequent financial trouble. It is really tough. It is truly hard. It is a raw, difficult experience and, I believe, one of life's greatest challenges.

How do you get through it? How do you keep going? For me, a distinct perspective became my turning point and my anchor. This Soul Essential provided me safe harbor under the storm of unemployment.

I had to pivot and find other value, meaning, and enjoyment in my life despite the loss of my career and many of the financial benefits that had been accumulated from it.

Do not get me wrong—I like creature comforts as much as anyone. I am not a minimalist. But I am saying that when you lose things in life such as a career, a job, a corner glass office, cars, your house, and maybe even awesome perks like fine dining, you need to shift the value you placed on those items and benefits to other things in life.

I had to Move My Mansion.

If you lose a brick-and-mortar mansion, you need to shift your value and love to another mansion.

Either the loss of a job and the financial
trouble that came with it would pull me
down or I could wrestle free from its clutches
to move on and find new success.

I am not perfect at adjusting and Moving My Mansions. It is hard. But I believe you and I can live above the hold these things can have on us and find happiness and fulfillment in life.

During my experience of unemployment, my wife and I took a day trip. The weather was beautiful, a bright sun against a deep blue sky. We decided to tour a historical mansion. It was our first visit.

The mansion was a depiction of very wealthy living in the 1800s. The mansion had expansive grounds and was inspiring with its architecture, several wings, and many rooms. It was built by brothers from England who had developed a successful business. Back in the day, the mansion was a hot spot of social festivities.

I distinctly recall the extensive grounds and impressive construction, all modeled after the great mansions that dot the English countryside.

In its time, the mansion was the socialite, who-is-who hot spot, and it was a public demonstration of the brothers' wealth. It was an obvious achievement to have built such a wealthy business and to have been able to construct and own such an impressive mansion.

Then came a poignant and unforgettable moment for me. I learned that the wealth of the brothers was significantly impacted in market downturns and that one of the brothers, considering himself bankrupt, took his own life. I stood in the mansion shocked by this story. It was raw and haunting. To me, the brother who died had much to live for. I cannot judge him, nor was I privy to all the contributing mental and emotional factors that culminated in the taking of his life. But it was believed that the loss of the mansion, the wealth, and all that I was seeing and experiencing were contributing factors.

Please think about this for a minute. I was standing in the middle of an amazing mansion, a very valuable obtainment surrounded by expansive grounds, the kind of grounds you would love to picnic at or visit to throw a ball for miles with a dog called Zeus. But were the grounds and the mansion more valuable than the life of this man?

I pondered how lifeless obtainments can hold such gravity upon our lives.

My thoughts summed into a key question: "Do I have the ability to choose happiness in financial loss as well as in financial good times?"

My answer is that I believe I do.

I realized that I had to Move My Mansion in order to come out on the other side of my hard unemployment experience successfully.

I had to find value and enjoyment in other pursuits in my life. To chart such a course is not easy—it may even be the challenge of a lifetime—but such direction, I believe, holds a priceless destination worth fighting for and protects your soul from projecting downwards.

This true Soul Essential lesson from the mansion made me think deeply about my reactions to my own downturn and, more importantly, determine where my personal mansion was.

> *The mansion had my admiration, but*
> *the story had my attention.*

More importantly, I left that day with a new commitment, a new approach, a new direction. It was this: I had to Move My Mansion. I had to be courageous, accept change and loss, react better, and progress with a different priority focus.

If this Soul Essential is for you, then decide today to find ways to Move Your Mansion. Remember, if you need to Move Your Mansion, you are not alone. I had to be soul strong and Move My Mansion in order to *Interview Strong*.

USE ADVERSITY TO YOUR ADVANTAGE

Many people I have worked with over the years who were unemployed or underemployed have found great benefit in the content of this next Soul Essential.

I know from firsthand experience that when I was in the crucible of my unemployment, the last thing I wanted to hear about was the silver linings of unemployment. But silver linings can be found in most clouds, including stormy unemployment clouds.

If I had understood Use Adversity to Your Advantage back in my time of unemployment, I would have found more contentment, developed more hope, and achieved a happier, positive attitude and perspective.

My mother used to say, "Every experience, positive or negative, is experience."

Indeed, the growth and development we achieve in our hard times give us the true dividend. There is growth that seems only possible through experience. I think that if you live an insulated life, your development will be less than what it could have been otherwise.

Alternatively, if your life has challenges, stretching experiences, and obstacles to overcome, you will be full of life's lessons and learnings. You will not be shallow. You will build up your capability. You will be more skilled, wise, experienced, and useful to industry and to others.

Most of us do not volunteer for this kind of growth because the needed experience often comes through hard knocks. Such challenging experiences often disrupt our plans, changes our course, and redefines our dreams. To gain such experience usually requires taking us to unforeseen destinations, brings us to new relationships, demands adjustment, deepens our perspective, and opens our eyes.

I have often seen those who have been unemployed look back on their experience and find advantages that added to their development, character, and capability.

To find that growth and development in the experience of employment challenges, I believe it is necessary to accept and recognize the position you are in.

That is, you are in a position that can grant you the unbeatable power of experience.

Over the years, I have identified the following markers from my own unemployment experience and from touch points with many others who have gone through their own employment trouble. I have built this list of the top development and growth markers that came from unemployment to help you.

If you are in the mindset to Use Adversity to Your Advantage, to turn a negative into a positive, you can increase your capability.

Again, I know being unemployed is extremely hard. But please let me summarize the development and growth markers I have learned over the years, that came to people through the adversity of unemployment.

Do not just skim through the list. Think about each one.

Select several development and growth markers from the list that you can adopt, internalize, and seek to personally develop. These will become part of the new you that will ultimately come out the other side of your unemployment challenge.

Here are the top personal development and growth markers:

- Developing courage within you where passiveness once reined.
- Accepting that office politics rule over talent and truth; and act upon fiction and watercooler philosophies.
- Finding out that you are enough when you lose your title, job, office, and more.
- Building new networks, you had never experienced before.
- Discovering the blessing of earning income and working to your potential. Many in the world do not obtain it.
- Learning that the promotion that passed you by became the rocket within you to move you to a better place.
- Exploring your newfound ability to manage more effectively from the corner office.
- Having a broader knowledge of industries and gaining new skills.
- Increasing in your admiration for work.

- Deepening your realization of your weaknesses so that they can become strengths.
- Accepting that the gift of work may not always be accompanied by the position we want but that work is still a gift.
- Finding unknown power within you to sacrifice in order to work and provide, including sacrificing ego, pride, and title.
- Finding a sincere realization of what is most important in life. It is not the office.
- Finding happiness and satisfaction in a different socioeconomic station.
- Deepening your gratitude. It is amazing what you become grateful for when work does not love you back.
- Developing real empathy for others, the kind of empathy that changes how you treat those around you.
- Finding in yourself ego you did not know existed and tempering it with humility.
- Eliminating your judgment of others' social and economic standing.
- Discovering that you can be kinder in life and stay that way.
- Learning that the joy of a day can be yours no matter your title or office size.
- Appreciating how special a new piece of clothing can be when the budget is tight.

- Adjusting your appetite so that your previous expensive taste can be satisfied with economic taste buds.
- Realizing that an office desk, once an unnoticed furniture piece, provides you with peace.

Use Adversity to Your Advantage to build capability.

Allow your experience to make you grow. I believe if you do not, it can have adverse effects. The experience will not bring out the best in you. Time will move on, and you may end your unemployment *without* the consequential development being woven into your character.

I want you behind a desk again or back in the factory or behind the wheel, but I want you there better than you were before you left—so that you can contribute more effectively.

One day in the future, if ever needed, I want you better tomorrow, than you were yesterday, so that you can *Interview Strong*.

KEEP MOVING BY APPLYING THE FIVE GS

When there is no job forcing you to get up in the morning, you can be lured into being idle. To me, idleness reduces your effectiveness. I recommend that you be productive every day. I believe it is important to protect your soul with this Soul Essential. It is not good for you to be down in down times. I think it is better for you to be up and doing regardless of whether you have a job offer or not.

I believe you are better off to get your "keep moving gear" on.

After my mansion moment and internalizing that lesson, it was time for me to get moving and keep moving. Hence my Soul Essential Five Gs.

The following are my Five Gs to keep moving:

1. Get Up Early
2. Get Moving
3. Get Applying and Practicing
4. Get Networking
5. Get Serving

Get Up Early: Set your alarm early in the morning Monday through Friday and get up. This will invigorate and energize your body and mind for the rest of the day. Aim to get up around 6:00 a.m. or earlier. You will be ahead of the game and be ready to work on the other four Gs.

Get Moving: I have learned that physical daily exercise is essential for those going through employment hard times. Plan an hour for this each day. Walking, jogging, swimming, cycling, aerobics, stair master, martial arts, boxing, and sports—whatever fits you, do it every day, of course under your doctor's care and supervision. We do not want any heart attacks! I believe it is important that you get moving every day and set goals for your own personal physical exercise program. Again, this is especially needed when you are enduring your own personal employment challenge.

Get Applying and Practicing: Monday through Thursday I recommend you try to find and apply each day to one high-fit job. That effort can produce up to four good applications a week. I am not talking about vanilla, easy, lazy applications. I am talking about robust, customized job applications. Here is the difference.

A vanilla, easy, lazy application looks like simply seeing a job posting, submitting a basic cover letter with your standard resume, and hoping for the best. No, no, no, that will not meet the bar. You need to find that job posting you want or can do, customize your resume against the job requirements, and write a customized cover letter. That is a sincere reach out for that job. Back it up with networking efforts.

Be Interview Ready, and I mean *really* Interview Ready.

To be Interview Ready, I believe you need to practice interview skills and techniques with a buddy or in the mirror for an hour each day, Monday through Thursday.

I also recommend you become great at designing an interview strategy and plan so that you are ready to draw upon your plan when an interview comes.

Practice delivering powerful and timely Hit Backs and Double Punches and seek to be proficient in your Directional Targeting.

What about practicing Tough Questions? Get to a master level where no interview question or scenario will scare you.

In my experience, you should be interview tough and should interview smart in order to *Interview Strong*. Set aside practice time on your calendar for an hour each day, Monday through Thursday, to get Interview Ready.

Get Networking Inside: Set aside an hour or two each day Monday through Thursday for Networking Inside. Before you apply for a job, as part of your daily networking, focus on finding key people in the company, or in its supply chain, or in the industry. Your networking time will hopefully produce someone to include in your cover letter or resume or someone who could put in a good reference.

You can also Network Inside for knowledge to utilize in your application and interview. Through networking, you can seek to job shadow in the company to which you have applied, with another company in the industry, or in the company's supply chain.

What has really helped me with my Networking Inside efforts is to view the company to which I have applied, both vertically up and horizontally across the entire industry and supply chain.

This is a strategic approach to Networking Inside. Do not limit your networking efforts to the company to which you have applied.

Think of people you could contact in the supply chain—the market, competitors, suppliers, vendors, customers, and all employees of potential integrations and interdependencies surrounding the company. This strategic approach to networking significantly expands your opportunities to connect with relevant people. I share a powerful experience in the Network Inside chapter, on when networking the supply chain resulted in me getting my first job, a great job, following graduation from college.

If you sit down for several hours a week and focus purely on networking, the results may surprise you. Research websites and industry trends, make phone calls, or pay a visit to a key person who can help you learn more or provide an edge to your application. Job shadow or get inside some other way. Or maybe it would be good to commence a course or certification that will support your application. Education and certification are also part of networking. These are just a few key suggestions to effectively use your networking time.

Get Serving: Set aside some time to serve others each week. This can include spending time with family, giving personal service to others, volunteering in the community, guest lecturing, visiting the sick in hospital, performing charity work, or giving back in numerous ways. I cover this topic more extensively in chapter seventeen.

Friday: What is happening on Friday? Friday is an awesome day. You still get up early, and you still get moving physically, but on this day, you Treat Yourself to something special.

This is your special treat day. I cover the power of Treating Yourself in chapter seventeen. For now, I want you to simply plan out your week and include Friday as a day off from applications; set the day aside as treat day. Treating Yourself reminds you that you are valuable and special. I believe treat day, especially when you are unemployed or underemployed, reinforces your dignity and self-worth.

In my experience, if you apply the Five Gs each week, your unemployment experience will exponentially improve, and the Five Gs will help lift you up. They will help strengthen your soul and skills to empower you to *Interview Strong.*

SOUL ANCHORS II

In the day-to-day adversity of employment hard times, your soul needs to stay ahead of the game, and remain resilient in order to *Interview Strong*.

CHAPTER SEVENTEEN

SOUL TACTICS

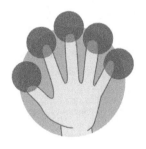

Soul Tactics are designed to be your anchor, to strengthen your soul. I have authored them with the intent that they provide a focus on what you do and how you act and react under the adversity of employment challenges.

A lion cannot hunt effectively, with a thorn in its paw.

In my experience, Soul Tactics will help protect you from soul inhibitors, the thorns that can puncture your job search paws.

I firmly believe that if you keep and align with Soul Tactics, you will be able to *Interview Strong*.

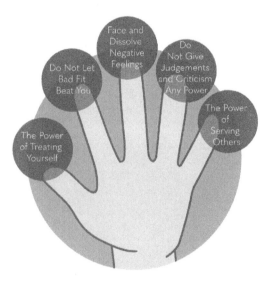

THE POWER OF TREATING YOURSELF

In my experience, it will take on average several months to source and find a new job and even longer to get that promotion. Add more months for higher salaried jobs. It takes time, resume, and interview preparation. It takes hard work. It is a full-time job to find another job. Do not be excessively hard on yourself if success does not come immediately or as quickly as you would like. Be persistent.

I have personally experienced and have witnessed the power of the Soul Tactic of Treating Yourself when enduring unemployment.

Say what? Yes, I believe you need to take some time to regularly Treat Yourself.

You need to consistently strengthen your dignity, value, and self-worth.

I recommend to those who I am coaching that they take time to live this Soul Tactic. I believe it is vital. In my experience, Treating Yourself will improve your job applications and will greatly enhance your interview skills. Why? Because Treating Yourself reinforces your true dignity, independent value, and self-worth in the face of job application rejections and in living through the day-to-day hardships of unemployment.

When your human dignity is on trial under the adversity of unemployment, you need to strengthen it.

This might sound like a strange recommendation to Treat Yourself to something special when unemployed. The average human reaction when experiencing difficulties with employment is to not indulge.

The average feeling is not being worthy of a treat, or gravitating to the couch to wallow, or shrinking into the underemployed mold the office tells you that you should be in.

Others react by going into a fierce, total work mode, leaving no time for treating themselves until after regaining employment.

> *Treat Yourself, even though you may be*
> *unemployed or underemployed.*

Again, I have seen many times that Treating Yourself reinforces your dignity, even though your neighbor just bought a new car, and you cannot. Or even worse, your car just got repossessed. Or Jimmy just got promoted even though you and the entire office know he is an idiot. Or your bills are mounting up and you feel like a loser.

> *Treating Yourself helps provide inner protection*
> *against rejection and helps you to stay distinct*
> *and separate from your employment status.*

I have seen people implement so many varied and personal examples of this Soul Tactic as they have dealt with unemployment.

One man went out and purchased an expensive new tie. The shopping experience was a treat for him, and the new tie would give his interview presentation a boost.

Another candidate took some savings and purchased a membership at a spa and went regularly. Another would go out into nature for the day and have a picnic. For another, it was a treat to go to the movies. Sometimes, when finances are tough, it can be enough just to do something inexpensive but still special to you. It could be getting an ice cream sundae or going to a special place. Whatever it is, ensure that you Treat Yourself once a week.

This Soul Tactic will help your soul successfully survive unemployment and underemployment and ultimately prepare you to *Interview Strong*.

DO NOT LET BAD FIT BEAT YOU

I once received a job offer, a promotion to an account manager position. It was more money and seniority, but it required a relocation. We were so excited, but the excitement was short-lived. I was not in the job very long before I realized that the lure of the promotion had obscured my vision of the reality of my fit to the position.

I needed an empowering Soul Tactic to navigate this employment challenge. I confess I was a terrible account manager. Managing accounts was not me. I hated it, and I was not good at it. The company culture was not a good fit for me either. Management quickly became aware of my inadequacies, and the scrutiny upon me intensified. I, in turn, overcompensated to try to right my sinking ship. But inevitably, the ship was going down, and I needed to find a lifeboat. I will admit, it was embarrassing. The growing water cooler whispers regarding my account management competencies were not complimentary. Naturally, I was internalizing all of this to the point that I was not feeling very capable. My self-esteem was taking a hit.

I wish that I understood the Soul Essential of Maintain Your Distinction back then and that I had this Soul Tactic: Do Not Let Bad Fit Beat You. In any event, my future looked bleak, and the weather matched my mood. It was winter, and gray clouds blanketed the sky day after day.

The weather shifted in the spring, and the sun started to break through the clouds. During these sunlit days, I began to see myself differently.

I realized that I was not a bad performer, the real truth was that I simply was not a good fit.

> *Recognizing good or bad fit in a job is vital*
> *to preserving your dignity and self-worth—*
> *to not being deceived into thinking you*
> *do not have capability when you do.*

A bad fit in a job is like having to wear an ill-fitted baggy suit or jeans and a T-shirt three sizes larger than your size. Even worse, you must look at that bad fit in the mirror every day.

Remember that bad fit does not mean you are not good. Bad fit simply means you need to find the right size and cut of work clothes.

Shortly after that spring epiphany, I discovered opportunities in consulting and training. I loved it and found I could excel in that industry.

Think about that for a minute. Think about the power of it. I could have been deceived by bad fit, even to the point of not believing in myself. Do not be deceived by bad fit. Measure your true effectiveness by good fit. Do not let poor fit make you feel like you cannot be successful.

Do not let bad fit limit you.

Bad fit can be caused by many circumstances. One of them is having the wrong job.

Generally, it is the wrong place and the wrong time if you lost your job or got demoted due to bad fit.

Alternatively, what if your boss was threatened by you and wanted to keep you down? That is a compliment. Maybe your boss changed, and this new boss's friends were being onboarded while you were out boarded because you were not a groupie. Or maybe there was a culture shift, and you were shifted out. Either way, it can all amount to bad fit. To me, many of these business decisions are arbitrary and political at best. Therefore, it is generally a mistake to take changes in your employment as a sign of your limited capability when in reality you were just not a good fit.

Unfortunately, sometimes employees and candidates are discriminated against. That is not bad fit; this is something more horrendous. Regrettably, discrimination is real.

I wish discrimination were eliminated from the workplace entirely, but it can creep in and influence employment decisions. That is very personal to your protected class. I believe discrimination is toxic and does not determine personal worth, nor is discrimination a good or appropriate basis to assess actual ability or talent upon. It is not only an ineffective selection filter but is also illegal as a basis for employment decisions. That is exactly what makes discrimination terrible.

Discrimination is not only against employment laws, but it is the worst basis for decision making, as discrimination does not have eyes to see real people, real talent, and true potential. The negative personal bias inherent in discrimination obscures decision makers' views of the true worth, talent, and ability of the human soul.

 The challenge, of course, is that discrimination can be difficult to prove. I have been asked what my advice is to anyone who feels that they have been discriminated against in employment. My immediate reaction is to encourage the victim to stand up against it and pursue all remedies.

Discrimination only condemns the perpetrator and exposes their lack of ability, not the person being victimized. Hold on to your value and abilities and move forward in positive and remedial ways if you have been discriminated against. Do all you can to stand up to and stamp out discrimination.

Back to bad fit. I have seen many people who were selected for downgrading or for termination due to bad fit who leave a company and go on to achieve great things in a different position or in another industry that was a superior fit for them.

Hence the power of this Soul Tactic: Do Not Let Bad Fit Beat You. Unemployment cuts wide for many reasons; bad fit can be one of those reasons.

> *The trouble with bad fit is that it is often hard to discern. It can be confusing. The difference between bad fit and your own capability can be hard to identify and accept.*

When it comes to judging your own performance, it is natural and normal, I think, to try to achieve the same as those around you. We also strive for recognition.

But at some point, in that journey, at some point in climbing up the social and performance curve, I think it is healthy to sit back and take a moment to determine your fit, to assess your natural talents and compatibility.

> *You may have to accept that you are just a round peck in a square hole and that you need to stop banging your head against a brick wall to make it happen.*

Remember the baggy suit and jeans. You are still great; you just need to go shopping and find better fitting work clothes, a cut and style of work clothes that will enable you to shine and to move forward to *Interview Strong*.

FACE AND DISSOLVE NEGATIVE FEELINGS

There is no holiday from unemployment or underemployment, and that is why you need this Soul Tactic. The emotional impact of unemployment or underemployment can be very penetrating.

Day after day during your employment challenge, your dignity is on trial.

The hardship is real, trust me, and those feelings can harden inside. I believe that it is so important for most people to have someone safe to talk to, to work through any hurt, feelings, mourning, loss, or trauma associated with unemployment and its financial and social impacts.

In my experience, it is very difficult to successfully progress through job interviews if there are unresolved feelings or emotions. These negative feelings can ooze out in the interview and block your ability to sell yourself with confidence. I have experienced firsthand and observed in others the impact unresolved feelings can have on interview capability.

Unresolved negative, sad, or embittered feelings can inhibit your confidence and expression and stop you from being able to Interview Strong.

I believe it both necessary and healthy to face and dissolve any negative feelings associated with your employment challenge. It is so important to get those feelings up and out.

Sometimes this can be achieved with someone you know and trust. Sometimes a professional counselor can help.

For me, I was months into my unemployment experience when I got the help I needed. It came via a phone call. The house had become claustrophobic, and the four walls locked me in as I worked each day on job applications and prepared for interviews. Ironically, in this position you long for the freedom work provides.

When the phone call came, it was a dark winter night. I took the call sitting on the couch in the front room, facing a window out to the garden. A trusted friend with counseling experience had called to check in on me. The fact that he had thought to call was touching, but the way he started the conversation was penetrating.

He said, "Mark, how are you really doing?" He then continued, "It must be very hard, day after day without work, living on your savings." He paused, and then ventured further, "So, how are you really doing?"

It was a wise, gentle invitation. A tender summons for me to get it all up and out.

> *My friend offered a saving reach to release my hurt feelings before they hardened inside.*

I was at an emotional crossroads. One road led to disclosure and healing. That road, I instinctively recognized, would require me to be emotionally vulnerable. The other road, a "safer" road, held zero vulnerability, with no disclosure or admittance to being hurt. Ironically, that road was alluring, even though I knew it would not heal my soul.

I glanced out at the garden. The flowers and trees were barely visible at night, their natural beauty shadowed. I admired that garden. The flowers and greenery were strategically planted, and during the light of day, the flowers and plants cavorted in unison, showcasing a natural brilliance of vibrant life and color.

But night had fallen, overshadowing the garden's natural ability to achieve its inherent ability to contribute where it was planted. I reflected on that scene for a moment. Then I had a realization.

> *I did not want to be dominated forever*
> *by my circumstances. I did not want*
> *to be like a garden at night.*

I wanted to be all I could be. I wanted to be like those flowers and plants during the day—living, vibrant, and contributing in my fullness to the garden of life.

I decided to take the vulnerable, hard, honest, raw road, and I seized the opportunity. I gripped the phone a little tighter, steeled my focus, and ventured to speak. Out came my emotions, feelings I did not even realize I had. The hurt and pain associated with the loss all came up and out. The sad feelings about our future, our troubles, our finances. The feelings about loss of friends, change in social status, all deeply buried, poured out. Feelings about rejection, that feeling of "no one wants me," the difficult job search moments, and the not being valued—it all came up and out.

The shallow "Why me?" stone skimmed across
the surface of a pond of self-reflection to
finally sink and fade away into acceptance.

My friend listened. We talked. My tears flowed. The call ended, and my friend was gone.

I was left staring out at the garden and the same four walls. But I felt different following that conversation. I felt free. I felt the best I had in months. It was such a healing moment for me.

There was more work to do in this area to clean out the emotional closet, but from that point on, my job interviews were different. I was more positive. The underlying feelings and emotions I had suspected were negatively affecting my job interviews were gone. I started to enjoy interviewing. I actually found interviewing fun and exciting. I started experimenting with different interview techniques and skills. It was exhilarating. I was no longer haunted as deeply by the day-to-day impacts of unemployment. It was not that the daily impacts were not present, but their hold upon me was far less.

Face and Dissolve Negative Feelings so that you can strengthen your soul and *Interview Strong*.

DO NOT GIVE JUDGMENTS AND CRITICISMS ANY POWER

This Soul Tactic is included to help you to defend against any arrows that may come your way. I include this Soul Tactic because you are likely to encounter negative criticisms, silent or sniper judgments, and even hurtful comments regarding your employment status. How will you handle this kind of experience?

*How will you react? I believe how you react
and how you respond are very important.*

For me, facing a decision about how to react to criticism was a surprise. I had enough on my plate in dealing with unemployment. I did not want to make the problems of others my problems. That would be a mistake.

I believe this kind of behavior, this "kick them when they are down" approach, is not based on any substance. It is usually just the chirping of an opportunist or the grating of an ignorant misjudgment. To me, this kind of criticism is driven by something else, by other feelings. From my experience, this kind of behavior can seed from many factors: prejudice, judgment, ignorance, pride, competitiveness, misperception, or past unresolved enmity.

Whatever the reason for these comments and judgments, if you are giving your very best to your employment situation, such statements are not based on truth.

Unemployment can place upon you an inherent vulnerability to judgment—the kind of judgment and bias that can be hard to swallow.

It can be very frustrating to deal with negative judgment and criticism when you are unemployed or underemployed. It is difficult because you are in a glasshouse, and those throwing the stones know it.

I was not naive to my position and how I looked, so it was hard to defend against the stones. This Soul Tactic, Do Not Give Judgments and Criticisms Any Power, is an insightful Soul Tactic, your protection tactic, against the stones.

I wish some people had been kinder and more supportive, but that's life. I understood the social dynamics, but I did not understand the behavior of kicking someone when they are down. How should you react? With anger? With a desire for revenge? By believing it and internalizing it?

All these reactions might be tempting, but I believe they are counterproductive to getting a job because such reactions will tax your focus, time, and emotion.

My experience taught me the best approach is to let such behavior pass right on by. I advise that you do not let the judgments and criticisms of others embroil you. To me, that will only weaken the strength you have built in your soul. Karma can be a real deal, so leave it to karma.

*Reacting and getting embroiled can impact
your interviewing capability. Do not make
the problems of others your problems.*

This Soul Tactic is designed to help you successfully manage judgments and criticisms and maintain strength in your soul. You need to *Interview Strong*. Therefore, in underemployment and unemployment, I believe the best course is to ignore the criticisms and judgments of others. Do not internalize them. Do not react to them. Let judgments and criticisms pass on by. Do Not Give Judgments and Criticisms Any Power.

THE POWER OF SERVING OTHERS

In my experience, the gravity inherent in employment challenges is strong and has the propensity to pull your focus inward. Under this G-force, it is easy to become very myopic. Often, being myopic can have negative consequences on your interviewing effectiveness. The best power I know to inoculate you from being highly myopic comes in serving others. Service can be a lifesaving way to escape out of your circumstances, and to look outward.

Looking back on my own experience, serving others did exactly that. Time to serve others forced me to look outward and to think of those around me. It saved me. I highly recommend that you look to help others, to lift those around you, or to spend some special time with those who need it. It is very cathartic. Such service experiences also brought happiness to me and my family and invited sunny rays into some hard days. Service can also be a strength to your networking. However, maintaining the sure and pure motive to just serve others is key.

Service opportunities can look like this:

- Spend special time with others.
- Volunteer with your favorite charity.
- Sit on a committee in a volunteer capacity.
- Assist in a local community project.
- Visit the sick.
- Put your professional skills to work for someone else in need.
- Lunch with someone you know who needs your help and support.
- Mentor a recent graduate.
- Clean the house top to bottom.
- Care for the garden of someone who cannot do it themselves.
- Assist in organizing a charitable event.
- Visit the lonely and aged.
- Job shadow for free with someone in an industry or job of interest.
- Guest lecture.
- Be a tutor.
- Remove a burden from someone in need.

You get the picture of this Soul Tactic. I believe the Power of Serving Others helps us stay healthy and balanced between our inward- and outward-focused perspectives. Service is also a potent addition for resume and network building but should not be the primary motive.

Please remember the five Soul Tactics in your day-to-day living. They are designed to help you navigate your employment challenge more effectively. Ultimately, I believe Soul Tactics can help you *Interview Strong*.

LESSONS FOR SUCCESS

Insights from the Five, who *Interviewed Strong* and won.
Boast about yourself in your resume and during
your interviewing. If you don't, who will?

CHAPTER EIGHTEEN

RETURN TO THE FIVE

I would like to return to the Five and continue their story. I thought it would be beneficial for you to hear from several of the Five in their own words. Names have been changed for privacy.

Bill had worked in the aviation maintenance industry most of his life and needed to change industries. I have heard that goal many times before; there is nothing new with a request for an industry jump. However, in this case, Bill had my undivided attention.

> *He told me he would literally die if he*
> *could not make an industry jump.*

Bill believed that his health had taken a beating from the chemicals utilized in aircraft maintenance. He expressed in all seriousness that he would die if he continued to work in that environment. He was sure the chemicals were killing him. He showed me the effects on his skin. I believed him. He and his wife were living in a basement and waiting for a miracle for a new job in a new industry.

Achieving an industry jump is no small feat. He was applying to jobs day and night. Bill said he needed someone who could help him. He told me that when he listened to me lecture, he knew that he had finally found someone who could really help him.

That was a nice compliment. However, I could not enjoy it for very long, as I was already consumed and concerned about how I could help Bill reinvent himself after he had been in the same industry for years. How could Bill change industries after spending so many years in the same space?

An industry jump is not easy. But it is not impossible, either.

I looked at Bill's resume. Not only was it a three out of ten resume, but it was also a very industry-specific resume. It would be a huge leap to get him to another industry with his current resume and with most of his years of experience in one industry.

Years of experience in the aviation maintenance industry, and he cannot stay in it. Heck! Who would hire him in a new industry?

For Bill, I utilized the You Matrix to find his new industry. The tool was able to unlock his experiences, find skill threads, and determine his new potential.

Using the outputs from the You Matrix, we determined a new career of process engineering and then drafted a new resume. The *Interview Strong* principle of "Resume: A Ticket to Interview or a Ride to the Shredder" was instrumental in building an awesome, customized resume for Bill. He also had to gain some new certifications to meet job criteria for new roles in process engineering, so he went to work and completed those certifications. Bill now looked amazing on paper and had the qualifications to back it up.

But how would he interview?

Bill practiced and applied the *Interview Strong* methodology in every interview. As time went on, Bill needed bearing up, and Soul Essentials and Soul Tactics were a great anchor for his soul. Armor Up and the Big T Factor were also crucial content for Bill to internalize and understand.

Bill would later execute Big T Factor principles at a hotel lunch interview to seal the deal for a job offer.

Bill also applied Let's Talk Money at the right time while the luncheon was winding down.

Bill and I had talked about being willing to relocate as part of Let's Talk Money. Bill was ready for the relocation discussion, and he nailed it.

Soon Bill and his wife were on a plane to a new job opportunity in a new industry.

Bill's journey is a powerful example to us all. He espoused real, raw courage in the face of some chilling, deadly adversity. I will always love Bill for his courage to change and his work ethic to get the job.

BILL'S STORY

"From my perspective, this work [*Interview Strong*] has changed the lives of the Five and will change the lives of anyone who uses the principles contained therein! I had worked for twenty-plus years in aviation on composites, aircraft structures, hydraulic systems, and avionics. I had also been our safety coordinator and was exposed to lean implementations. In the last year, my crew of around 100 had multiple deaths from different forms of cancer. I had some health issues, including skin problems that the dermatologist could not remedy.

"One day I had a feeling come over me that if I wanted to live, I needed to change careers.

"Soon the airline announced an early-out option, and I took it. This was in August, and my exit date was scheduled for the week before Christmas. Surely, I could find a job by then.

"I worked eight to ten hours a day and spent four hours a day looking for work. When Christmas came around, I did not have any prospects. We moved across the country from our house into my parents' basement.

"I started attending an employment services meeting at the college. I first met Mark at there. The school was hosting a job search seminar. They were teaching many aspects of searching for a job. Subjects included topics like the use of social media, interview skills, and how to start your own business.

"The class that changed my life was taught by Mark. His class was on interview skills. He started with a demonstration of how interviews work. Strangely enough, it started with a set of tennis balls. The interviewer, Mark, would ask a question and toss the ball to the person being interviewed, who would answer and toss the ball back. Like in a real interview, you want to answer quickly, making your answer look genuine, but sometimes the rushed answer is not what you really want to say. This is especially true if the questions increase in speed. Mark explained that the interviewer wants to pick the candidate who will reflect best on them. If instead of answering every question you turned the answer into a question, the interview then turned into a conversation. Having a conversation gives you the ability to build trust, and people who are trusted get the job. I knew at that moment that Mark could help me.

"After the class, I and others asked if Mark could help us find jobs. We had a private meeting, the five of us and Mark. He committed to help us find work, and we committed to learn from him and use what he taught us. The five of us continued meeting at the business college, but on the side, we were meeting with Mark.

"The first thing that Mark had me do was to rewrite my resume. I had thought it was good, but it achieved nothing, so it got rewritten. The new resume was sent out and, a few weeks later, I got an interview. I met with Mark, and we practiced how to interview. The next day I wrote a list of questions for the interview.

"My first interview was an hour and a half long with the global director of lean deployment. Thanks to Mark's help and ideas, it was an awesome experience and a wonderful conversation. We both learned about each other. It was my goal to have every question I could think of asked before the interviewer asked if I had any questions so that my response could be, 'I think I've asked them all, but is there anything that you think I might have missed?' It was six interviews and about five months later that I started work at that job."

Bill amazes me. He is a great example of perseverance.

May I now introduce you to Sierra. She was a sensitive person who had already undergone some hardships in her life.

Now she was dealing with unemployment.

Having been in sales in the paper industry for years, Sierra was struggling to gain employment. Downturns in that industry would make it hard to get employment in what she knew and did best, which was selling paper. The paper industry changes were driving Sierra to reinvent herself.

The time of unemployment and dealing with the unknown was taking a toll on Sierra's soul. Having the Interviewing Mindset, with an emphasis on gearing up with Soul Essentials and Soul Tactics, greatly helped Sierra get her soul ready to interview. Armor Up was key to building her interview skills and technique, and the Big T Factor really helped her to *Interview Strong*. Hit Backs and Double Punches empowered Sierra. It would not take long for her to **get that job**. Smart and confident, she was in a good position very quickly. The You Matrix enabled her makeover to achieve an industry jump. Let's Talk Money was crucial to helping Sierra seal a job offer. Within several months, Sierra was thriving in her new employment in a new industry! I was so proud of Sierra. She became strong, and she *Interviewed Strong*. Sierra is an amazing individual who adapted and continued to strive for something better. She never gave up until she achieved it.

SIERRA'S STORY

"Each time I read my story; I cry. Unemployment or underemployment can be traumatic. Mine should not have been. I was doing very well in my industry. I had been awarded for double-digit sales growth for a decade and was recognized by peers and customers.

For me, three unexpected deaths happened within weeks of each other—a parent, a spouse, and a job that was killed by a reduction in force. All this put me in a tailspin. But the job needed to come before I would ever consider myself ready. The pressure to find the perfect job was immense, and I struggled to visualize having an interview without crying.

"Mark was not afraid of my tears. There had been another coach who suggested that I go wash my face and toughen up. That coach I did not return to for help.

"Happens that there was a friend in my Fab Five story! My new friend had been an executive who aimed to replace her six-figure salary, and boy she could cry. I knew the unemployment emotions were not reserved for lightweights like me. Mark heard my pain as well as saw my determination weaken.

"When we began coaching with him, he had us all come in our finest dress to have a lunch meeting at one of the best hotels in town.

"As I recall what I wore, I remember that it was not my best. Oh, my nice clothes were in the closet, all right, but I did not feel like I could wear my power suits anymore, ever! Mark pulled no punches and taught us how to negotiate salary range without blushing.

"Over the weeks of checking in with Mark and the others, we had mock interview sessions. And since I was trying to identify a new industry, the resume adjustments felt like major surgeries versus facelifts to the accomplishments I was most proud of.

"It was time to move on. One interview went well before someone said something not very nice to me. It cracked my resolve, and I did indeed cry. It was inevitable, and I never needed to see them again! And I was glad it was over, like that Chinese tile game where the first instruction is to fail fast. Shocker, I did not get that job. But it was a successful milestone for me. I started wearing powerful clothes and brushing off the attitude of 'You should pick someone else.'

"At our final meeting with Mark, my friend and I returned to the same fancy hotel lobby to meet with Mark. We did not need the instruction of wearing our best. We greeted each other with confidence, laughter, and relief as we continued to use what we were learning from the chapters on Let's Talk Money and the *Interview Strong* technique.

"It took a few more months yet. I could tell that the power was ultimately not in the suit. But, until my confidence fully returned, I splurged and bought a new push-up bra to rock the attitude and the suit.

"My new job did not meet all my itemized accomplishments or certifications, but it brought relief and helped me recover, and I have since advanced into new responsibilities that utilize more of my strengths. I would have never chosen it. But I do love it now. Where is book two, Mark?! You got the job, now what? How to network. The guide to creating your new career path."

TINA'S STORY

Now, let us meet Tina. She had years of experience on systems projects in the IT industry, but the long hours and project milestones had been all-consuming. She told me she had lost her life in her work. It is funny how that can happen.

Burned out, but highly skilled, Tina had enough. A toxic environment by management was the final straw. She bailed. I cannot blame her. I do not know if she was thinking of a sea change when she bailed or if she planned on returning to the lucrative IT industry, but full marks to Tina for voting with her feet.

The You Matrix provided a great starting point. Once applied, it was very telling for Tina. The You Matrix was pointing her to return to her old industry. On the emotional side, acceptance of what had occurred at her past job was instrumental to moving forward and Soul Essentials and Soul Tactics were key. Resume -Ticket to Interview or Ride to the Shredder, and Let's Talk Money were pivotal for Tina. Experienced and savvy, Tina quickly adapted to the *Interview Strong* methodology and executed Hit Backs, Double Punches, and Directional Targeting highly effectively. She received an offer within several months.

According to the latest update, Tina is now a top consultant. I will always love Tina for her tenacity and ability to move forward. She was and is brave and did not let bad treatment or past challenges hold her back.

SAM'S STORY

Then there was Sam. I will always remember his brown glasses and searching eyes. Sam was the most introspective and emotionally transparent person I have ever worked with. I love his character and attributes.

Unemployment had really hurt Sam. His heart was pained by it. I gently reached out and touched his heart, and out poured the emotions. The cathartic release was so enabling for him and facilitated his readiness to interview. All *Interview Strong* chapters were applied. Sam was an amazing trooper under the trial of unemployment. I remember his "I got the job" phone call. What a celebration! When I think of Sam, I think of persistence. Sam was resilient. As of the last update, Sam is doing well in the benefits compensation industry. Sam was brave in the dark and pressed on, no matter what, to conquer a new terrifying world we casually call unemployment.

Lastly, may I introduce Darrell. He was a tall, thin man and thrived in the editing and writing space. The financial impact of unemployment on his family weighed heavily on him.

To me, Darrell worried more about the impact of unemployment on his family than he did about his own well-being. He worked so hard with me to get that job. Time was of the essence. I applied all the *Interview Strong* content. For him, a resume make over, Psychology of Waiting and Tough Questions were key.

I recall one day when there was an issue with his resume. Darrell had spent all afternoon completing his resume and cover letter and was excited to apply to a new job opportunity and head out the door for a Friday night event. I had to rain on his parade.

"No, you cannot send this in," I strongly asserted into the phone. "You need to customize the resume to the job application, or it'll be shredded."

The silence on the other end was tangible.

"It won't make it past human resources," I urged. I knew it would mean hours of more work for him. I knew it would derail his Friday night plans. It was a moment of impasse. He relented. He thanked me later.

I loved Darrell for his selflessness and the love he had for his family. He pushed ahead for them. Looking after his family was his priority. He faced his unemployment foes and did whatever it took. He was a great example of the power of love—how love can strengthen you and how it can get you through anything.

DARRELL'S STORY

"All of us were going through a rough time, some more than others. The day we met Mark was a big turning point for me. We gathered in a circle and Mark told us his story. He really gets it. He really understands. Nothing he shared was theoretical. It was *very real*. Mark understands! What a very emotional and sobering experience. What a relief!

"One day I sent Mark my resume, which I had prepared with a lot of effort. I was particularly proud of this resume! When we spoke on the phone, he bluntly stated something like, 'Your resume is going to cause disaster.' That hurt. It knocked me flat. Once reality hit me, I realized my pride had to go out the window. Mark was right, and how grateful I was for the resume makeover he coached me through.

"One day I had a *really* important job interview, and Mark and the five of us met for lunch. I mentioned my pending interview with the group. Mark said, in his matter-of-fact style, 'You need to wear a blue dress shirt, and it needs to come from Nordstrom's.' I replied, 'Well, I have a nice green shirt.' Mark replied, 'That won't do. It has to be blue and come from Nordstrom's.'

"Sierra immediately offered to take me to Nordstrom's. Bill offered to drive me to the interview. We went shopping. Sierra insisted on buying me a nice blue shirt and a yellow tie, the most expensive I have ever owned. Bill drove me to my interview. I felt so much more confident, and even though I did not get that job, my perspective had changed about how taking care of me first really mattered. Later that day I called Mark and the others to report on my interview and thank each one of them for their encouragement and belief in me. I felt so grateful!

"Believe in yourself. Believe that things will get better. They really will. You are not alone in this employment journey. Things will work out.

"Mark coached me on the *Interview Strong* methodology, dramatically improving my resume and interview preparation and delivery skills. This made a tremendous difference in more ways than one. My confidence skyrocketed, and my ability to present myself on paper and in person gained previously unknown clarity and precision. I was prepared like never before!

"Today, thanks to Mark and other blessed souls who crossed my path, I have the best job ever in my life working as a senior editor for a large engineering firm. I am so grateful!"

A TIME TO CELEBRATE

After each of the Five had received a job offer, we all gathered for a special celebration dinner. They had each earned the title of being the Awesome Five and the Courageous Five. In their own way, each one of them was incredible to me. At our celebration dinner, they looked so different from the Five I had met months prior. New jobs had brought light to their faces and placed a bounce in their step.

This was the first time we had all been able to gather since our initial meet and greet months prior.

I asked the Five what they had learned from their experience. How had they developed through it? They each outlined a personal development gain from their respective journeys. I listened in admiration at the respective increases in capability that each one had acquired from their experience of unemployment. It was a very inspiring moment.

Humanity really can rise above challenging moments and successfully make it through employment hard times.

Each day had been filled with hard work. I would call each of them three to four times a week for coaching sessions, for review and preparation. I had known them through their bad days, through their downtimes, through their up times, and through their fears and doubts. But tonight, was a time to celebrate.

As the night was ending and we left the dinner, I reveled in the newfound confidence in the walk and in the upbeat demeanors of each of the Five.

The faces of the Five displayed optimism. They had a bounce in their step. They had jobs. They had places to be tomorrow. Most importantly, someone wanted them—and they had rediscovered their self-worth. The Five had *Interviewed Strong* and won.

CHAPTER NINETEEN

IT'S OKAY TO BOAST ABOUT YOURSELF

In chapter on resumes, I mentioned the true story of Taylor. She was fantastic. Taylor had worked hard on her grades and had obtained several additional internships. She had a high GPA and had gained solid work experience which resulted in some great achievements. I was impressed. But her resume did not showcase this, and neither did her interview technique. Taylor was very reserved in representations of herself and what she had achieved. This was not new to me. I have seen this very frequently with college graduates.

I think it is an adjustment, a needed calibration to talk with confidence in the corporate environment and to sell yourself.

I stopped her at one point and said honestly, "Look, you have a great GPA, and you have achieved great things. You hold wonderful work experience and have some amazing achievements. But here is your issue in getting a job: If you do not boast about yourself in your resume and interviews, who will?"

She paused and reflected.

I pushed further, "You need to sell yourself."

I said, "The days of being the radiant college student are over." She really listened to me. I politely but firmly pressed further, "You need to go after it, because if you do not, the great "they" will give the job to someone else who will, and that would be a real shame because you are worthy of so much more. So do not shortchange yourself. You need to boast. You have earned it."

Taylor came back to me the next day and explained that my point had really hit home and that she had thought a lot about it throughout the night. Taylor decided to change this about herself going forward. What a champion Taylor is!

Your resume and interview are really platforms for you to sell yourself to get the job.

When you are job searching you can fall into a subtle but understandable mindset and approach of interviewing well as opposed to interviewing to get the job. There is a big difference.

The difference is discernable in how you answer questions and how you move forward in the interview.

You need to harness your hunger for the job and show it and vocalize it in the interview by really demonstrating that you want and are the perfect fit for the job. Are you there to interview, or to really get the job?

I always try to help those I coach focus on interviewing to get the job as opposed to just interviewing well.

One candidate I was working with asked for a refresher course after not achieving success. His new resume was netting many interviews, but he was not achieving job offers.

I interviewed him. My diagnosis was that he was not *Interviewing Strong.* He was interviewing well—to achieve high marks, to perform satisfactorily—but his focus had shifted from getting the job to interviewing perfectly. I said, "To me, you are not really going after the job in the interview. You are going through the motions instead."

I think this delicate difference is caused by the fact that there is safety from rejection and a sense of fulfillment in going through the motions as opposed to really going after the job with all your heart and energy!

I also noticed this candidate had lost his confidence and would look everywhere else but at the interviewer when answering the questions. I said, "I want you to maintain solid eye contact with the interviewer when answering. Do not look away. Be sharp and shorter in your responses and raise your voice. You are being mouse-like when you need to be a lion." I reminded him that the jobs he was applying for were management jobs, and so interviewers would be looking for attributes of leadership and confidence.

I also suggested a change from a gray shirt and blue tie to a white shirt and red tie. I wanted him to pop and showcase strong leadership.

It was only several interviews later that this client got a great job offer.

This is another example and approach to ensure you boast about yourself and step up, putting your best foot forward no matter what. Selling yourself with strength to do the job is a vital part of *Interviewing Strong*.

A POWERFUL PRINCIPLE

Hold on to this lifesaver during
employment hard times.

CHAPTER TWENTY

THE INHERENT POWER OF OPPOSITION

I want to leave you with a very powerful principle I learned from my mother—and remember, mothers are always right.

This lifesaver has helped me over the years and has ultimately held true for me. In the middle of life's storms, I have always tried to capture the vision and wisdom inherent in this principle. In doing so, I have discovered hope and a reason to persevere in dark times.

If you are having a tough time getting a job; if the days are hard, the opposition great, the challenges difficult, no imminent solution in sight; if you look in the mirror and think no one will hire me, please hang on to this one, hope-filled principle.

Our opposition is equal to our thrust forward.

I believe the degree of negative trouble we currently experience; will be equal to the degree of positive thrust forward we will have.

I consider this principle a law of nature. I believe, in time, you will land in a better job or a better place. Or maybe you will find and go in unforeseen directions that will ultimately be better for you.

Just because you cannot see the end in the dark does not mean that the end will not leave you better off in some way.

You cannot always count improvement in dollars, nor does improvement happen immediately, but I believe you can count on it in some way, especially if you are going through a tough time. Keep going. Keep striving.

I believe the negative opposition in your life will eventually reward you with an equivalent positive.

I sincerely hope *Interview Strong* has been and will be a great asset for you and help you to **get that job**.

One day you might interview me for a job, or I you. Either way, we might get that job, or we might not. But I would want both of us to have given it our all, to have given it our very best. I would want each of us to have *Interviewed Strong*.

Made in the USA
Monee, IL
05 June 2022

97541248R00184